T0171356

# The Day CHRIST Died as OUR PASSOVER

## A Harmony of Events at the Death of Christ with the Annual Jewish Passover

**This Bible Study Will—**

► Enrich our Appreciation of the Divine Arrangement in Redemption.

► Demonstrate the Flawless Consistency of the Biblical Record.

► Explode the Traditional Chronology of Christendom.

► Strengthen the Christian's New Freedom in Christ.

## JACK W. LANGFORD

WESTBOW
PRESS
A DIVISION OF THOMAS NELSON

Notes and a chart on this subject were first distributed in 1984. A fuller edition was
distributed and posted on an internet website in 1996. The first edition in book format was
made and posted on an internet website in 2007. This final edition is published in 2013.

WestBow Press books may be ordered through booksellers or by contacting:

WestBow Press
A Division of Thomas Nelson
1663 Liberty Drive
Bloomington, IN 47403
www.westbowpress.com
1-(866) 928-1240

ISBN: 978-1-4497-9308-1 (sc)
ISBN: 978-1-4497-9307-4 (hc)
ISBN: 978-1-4497-9309-8 (e)

Library of Congress Control Number: 2013910052

Printed in the United States of America.

WestBow Press rev. date: 06/20/2013

# CONTENTS

# *PREFACE*

M any years ago the book, *The Day Christ Died* by Jim Bishop, became a best seller. The year was 1957. The book seemed to remain popular for a good while. Jim Bishop was a news journalist who did extensive research, adding a flourish of conjectured novelty to make the event seem a more realistic drama by today's society. After all, concerning this day, he said it was *"The most important day in the history of the world."* In addition, Roman Catholic authorities also thought his book was important since Mr. Bishop followed their traditional scenario of a Friday crucifixion, making sure that the mother of Jesus was often tactfully situated. Consequently, the clerical authorities placed their nihil obstat and imprimatur on that particular script.

Of course, this day is vitally important spiritually to me as well, as it should be to every Christian. It was, in fact, *the day I died* in the person of my Substitute. The apostle Paul explained our supernatural identification with Christ in God's plan of redemption—"I have been crucified with Christ; it is no longer I who live, but Christ lives in me" (Galatians 2:20). It has been said that this passage is the one verse autobiography of every Christian. Unless a person has been "crucified with Christ" and also "risen with Him," he is not a Christian (see also Romans 6:1-11). Again Paul said "God forbid that I should boast except in the cross of our Lord Jesus Christ, by Whom the world has been crucified to me, and I to the world" (Galatians

6:14). This amazing identification takes place when one places his true heart faith in Christ as Savior and Lord.

Historically, the subject of the day Christ died began to be hotly debated a few hundred years after His death. In the council of A.D. 325 the leaders of the Roman "Imperial Church" thought it to be in the best interest of the church to disassociate their ritual observance of the death and resurrection of Christ, which they now called "Easter," away from the annual Jewish Passover event. They actually wanted to divert attention from the *Jewishness* of Jesus. In doing so, these "fathers" guided Christendom away from the Biblical reality as expressed by Paul—"Christ our Passover was sacrificed for us" (1 Corinthians 5:7). This error has been locked into their celebrations for over 1600 years not only by Roman Catholics but also by most Protestants.

This book, *The Day Christ Died as Our Passover*, is a fresh study that will have some surprises for most students of the subject. It will realign the death of Jesus Christ squarely upon the Biblical setting of the Passover theme as presented in the Scriptures. It will demonstrate beyond any shadow of a doubt that the four Gospels harmonize perfectly on the subject. It will establish the fact that Christ died precisely on the eve of Passover when the Passover lambs were being sacrificed in the Temple services.

I believe that, if you are a Christian, you cannot help but spiritually rejoice in this truth as you read through this material slowly and patiently. It has been gathered from a survey of the Hebrew Scriptures, from a proper harmony of the four Gospel records and also from outside historical records which have actually long been available. The conclusion will glorify the Lord Jesus Christ, God's provision for all mankind.

Jack W. Langford

# INTRODUCTION

"**D**id not our hearts burn within us while He talked with us on the road, and while He opened the Scriptures to us?" (Luke 24:32). These were the words of the two disciples on the road to Emmaus who had listened to a stranger who turned out to be none other than the Lord Jesus Christ, Himself (the text says they had been prevented from recognizing Him, verse 16). Truly, their hearts had been stirred as this stranger opened to them the beautiful truths from the Hebrew Scriptures which spoke of the very things which had happened to Jesus Christ in His sufferings, death and glorious resurrection.

Many of us, who have taken refuge from the judgment of God under the bloodstained doorposts of the cross of Jesus Christ, know exactly what these disciples experienced, as we have also read or heard explained the beautiful fulfillments of the Scriptures, especially in their expressive and inspired typologies. I remember vividly one such experience back in 1953, in a class I had taken in a Bible College I was attending. That class involved explorations of certain types of Christ from the Hebrew Scriptures. The instructor had given a very simple and yet very beautiful explanation of the Passover typology. It was the first time in my young Christian life I had ever heard anything like it; I was deeply stirred by its beauty.

God's final judgment upon Pharaoh and the Egyptians was announced beforehand by Moses to the Egyptians. However, most of them would not heed the warnings. God would destroy the firstborn son of all the households of Egypt with the exception of those who applied the blood of a young lamb or goat upon the doorposts of their houses. The children of Israel complied with God's directives. This event would mark a new national beginning for the people of Israel and their liberation from horrible bondage. On the 10th day of this first month every household was to select a lamb. It must be an unblemished male of the first year. They were to keep it until the 14th day and slaughter it in the afternoon of that day. The lamb would be roasted with fire, all of it to be eaten that evening with unleavened bread and bitter herbs. The bitter herbs were to be eaten as a remembrance of their bitter bondage in Egypt. Not a bone of that lamb was to be broken. Prior to going into their houses that evening they were to apply the blood of the lamb to the doorposts and lintels of their houses. Then they were not to venture out until the morning. God would pass through Egypt that night and an angel would strike with death the firstborn son of every household where the blood had not been applied. Where God saw the blood applied to the doorposts of the houses, He would "pass over" and exempt the firstborn of that home, not allowing the "destroyer" (Exo. 12:23) to strike that firstborn with death. This event would be a memorial for all generations to come. That night there was a "great cry" throughout the land of Egypt as the firstborn sons of the Egyptians died. All this can be read in Exodus chapters 11, 12 and 13.

In "the fullness of times" Christ came (Gal. 4:4). All four Gospels unite in placing the substitutionary sacrifice of Jesus Christ squarely in the middle of Israel's Passover celebrations of A.D. 30. In addition, special note is taken in the Gospel of John to the effect that "not a bone of Christ was broken" (John 19:36) in fulfillment of Exo. 12:46. Like Egypt of old, the world today ignores the warnings of eternal judgment. But God has provided a Lamb (the Lord Jesus Christ) Whose blood can be applied to the doorposts of their hearts by faith. Where such is done—God "sees the blood of the Lamb" and exempts that person from eternal condemnation. That person is also wonderfully delivered from the horrible bondage of sin to walk in new life in Christ.

When I first heard this story I was deeply stirred by the parallelism and the beautiful fulfillment in Christ. The Passover was revealed through Moses some 1500 years before Christ came to earth, fulfilling it in incredible clarity as the basis of salvation for all mankind. Like the men on the road to Emmaus (Luke 24:32), my own heart was, indeed, "burning."

However, the one additional thing that made this event so memorable to me was a problem or question that came up which reflected upon the subject. It actually brought a sudden disappointment in my appreciation of the subject; it caused me to slip from a spiritual "high" to a spiritual "low." The instructor had concluded by briefly explaining the *incongruity* of the commemoration of Christ's death on "Good Friday" in the modern Easter tradition with the actual Passover chronology at that time. In Christendom's traditional explanation of the event, Christ was crucified on *the day after* the annual Passover sacrifice of the lambs; then He was raised from the dead only a day and a half later on Sunday morning. The instructor explained that theologians had yet to solve that enigma which seemed to be insurmountable.

Right then and there, I purposed to find out why this "glitch" existed between the Biblical record of Christ's death and the modern traditional understanding of that Biblical record. I was not really overly obsessed with the issue because the overwhelming evidence of the truth was clearly stated by the apostle Paul, *"Christ our Passover has been sacrificed for us"* (I Corinthians 5:7). The apostle Paul was inspired to superimpose the sacrifice of Christ precisely upon the Passover event. The evidence of the typology was simply too beautiful to be discounted by a question in the actual chronology of the day of Christ's death, which has been magnified by later traditional additions and corruptions of Easter. However, today's critics of the Bible have continually pointed to the so-called "contradiction" in the Biblical record with apparent glee; they needed to be answered in a positive way.

Therefore, through the following years, amounting to several decades, as relative subjects came my way I placed them in my file on the subject. In the process of time, with a prayer in my soul for reliance upon the illumination of the Holy Spirit and a much better understanding of the Scriptures, the spiritual "low" on that issue was entirely erased, all thanks to God, through our Lord Jesus Christ. Like those two disciples on the road to Emmaus, my heart, and I hope yours also, will be thrilled all over again as we study this subject.

One further statement I wish to make. The apostle Paul, in talking about Christ as *"Our Passover,"* made it very clear that the one way believers in Christ can "keep the Feast" in its spiritual reality was to *"clean out the old leaven, that we may be a new lump"* (1 Cor. 5:7, 8). In the case of Paul's statement to the Corinthians, the "old leaven" was in the form of serious sexual immorality. In our modern age, however, the "old leaven" is primarily in the form of serious "spiritual immorality." The religious whoredoms of "Mystery Babylon" (Rev. 17) have spread from the very beginning of the creation of the "Imperial Church" in A.D. 313. Soon after in A.D. 325 the theologians of that generation legislated a mixture of Christianity and paganism to create their "Easter" celebrations. Thus, the ritual celebration in Christendom of Christ's redemption and resurrection has become a pollution of the Biblical record and of spiritual reality. Before the godly kings of Judah, Hezekiah and Josiah, could celebrate a renewed *"Passover,"* they had to clean out the leaven of religious idolatry which had polluted for Israel the glorious realities of the God-given Feast day (see 2 Chron. chapters 29-30 and 34-35).

As you will note in this study, I believe that the traditional celebrations centered around the Easter observations are one of the greatest hindrances to understanding the beauty of the subject more than any other factor. Likewise, the misunderstandings of those early clergyman in the "Imperial Church" have been perpetuated and magnified through the centuries. Consequently, in this study I will ignore certain traditions and focus upon a rediscovery of the amazing accuracy and beauty of the Scriptural revelation.

Jack W. Langford, April 2-3 (Passover), 2007

## Types and Antitypes

Some readers may not be familiar with the meanings and uses of these terms, *type* and *antitype*. Since I will be using these words frequently in this particular Bible study, it has been suggested that a further explanation of their Biblical origin, usage and importance would be helpful.

The writers of the Greek Scriptures (commonly called *The New Testament*) often looked back in their accounts to specific persons, objects and events found in the Hebrew Scriptures and explained them as *types, examples* or *patterns* which foreshadowed present realities to be realized by the Christian communities.

A few illustrations will suffice to demonstrate this. The apostle Paul spoke of "Adam, who is a *type* (Greek, *typos*) of Him (Christ) Who was to come," in Romans 5:14. Paul explained that just as Adam stood as the head of earth's naturally born family, so it is that Christ stands as the Head of the regenerated family of God. Then Paul made other comparisons and even some contrasts which also demonstrated a remarkable parallelism between the two heads of families. In another case, Paul wrote to the Corinthian assembly which was having many serious problems. Paul explained to them the experiences of the people of Israel in their wilderness journey and the troubles that befell them. Paul then specified that what happened to Israel served as "our *examples* (Greek, *typos*), to the extent that we should not lust after evil things as they also lusted" (1 Cor. 10:6). Again, Paul stated in verse 11 of this same chapter, "These things happened to them (Israel) as *examples* (Greek *typikos*)."

So we understand Biblical *types* as referring to examples, patterns, or models. The common idea is that of resemblance, similarity or correspondence. The person, object or event in the Hebrew Scriptures (commonly called the Old Testament) was designed to be a pattern or example for another person, object or event designated in the Greek Scriptures.

Jesus Christ, Himself, gave one of the most startling illustrations of the value of this type of explanation about important things. In Christ's famous discussion with the Jewish leader named Nicodemus (John 3:1-21), He explained the way of salvation and the new birth this way:

> And as Moses lifted up the serpent in the wilderness, even so must the Son of Man be lifted up, that whosoever believes in Him should not perish but have eternal life (John 3:14-15).

No doubt this was a startling revelation to Nicodemus. Though Christ stated this principle in brief words with a simple illustration, nevertheless it gave Nicodemus a lot to consider. In fact, it has given many theologians a lot to think about ever since Christ made the analogy. Probably no one would have given a second thought to the account where Israel was plagued by an apparent migration of venomous snakes out in the wilderness. Yet now, Christ drew our full attention to that event and used it as a picture of His own death and how one can be saved for all eternity. Had it not been for Christ's direct reference to this event, it would probably have remained dormant as an unimportant episode in Israel's history. Now, however, seeing the importance Christ gave to it, Bible students look with extreme carefulness at the story. After all, how to obtain salvation is an issue of supreme importance.

In reviewing the story (Num. 21:4-9) we note that Israel had rebelled against God at this stage in their journey. As a consequence God allowed serpents with a burning lethal bite to invade their camp. The poison which infected their bodies killed many of them and caused thousands of others to cry out for forgiveness and help. One knowledgeable about the original fall of man can easily see that this *typifies* what has happened to the whole human family. A *serpent* originally beguiled Adam and Eve (Gen. 3:1). As a consequence of Adam's sin and rebellion, the whole human family was infected by the "*old serpent,* the Devil" (Rev. 12:9). The poison of sin, which brings certain death (see Romans 7:17-20), entered into mankind's constitution. We then ask, "What could save the Hebrew people from physical death, and in turn, what can save humanity from a cruel eternal death in separation from God?"

God's instruction to Israel was to make a serpent of bronze or copper and hang it upon a pole to be lifted up for viewing by the people of Israel. Whenever a Hebrew was bitten he was merely to come and "look" (Num. 21:8) upon the serpent and thus be healed of the deadly snake bite. That was an amazing provision in God's grace. And now, according to Christ, what does God require of fallen mankind?—only to take a look of faith—"believe on" the Lord Jesus Christ Who was lifted up to hang upon the cross for all our sins. From this revelation we understand that salvation is not obtained from some complicated ritual or moral achievement; rather, according to Christ, salvation is simply obtained by an act of faith in the One Who bore all our sins.

But, many have instinctively asked, "How could an evil *serpent* ever typify the perfect, sinless Son of God?" This can only be answered by the realization that when Christ died upon the cross all the sins of the world had been placed upon Him. The Scripture says "God made Him (Christ) Who knew no sin to be **sin** (a *serpent,* if you please) for us . . ." (2 Cor. 5:21). When God judged *sin* in the person of our Substitute, we sinners were judged (Romans 6:6 and 8:3). By such substitutionary death, Jesus Christ, Himself, bore the power of the venom and "abolished death" for all who trust in Him (2 Tim. 1:10).

Thus, in this analogy the serpent hung upon the pole was the *type;* Jesus Christ hung upon the cross was the *antitype.* In addition, the Israelites merely "looking upon the serpent" were the second *type;* those persons "believing upon Christ" are the *antitypes.*

When one looks and realizes the simplicity—and yet the power and depth—of this phenomenal typology, the Scriptures will virtually come alive with deeper meaning and appreciation. In fact, the long known history of this typology has even left its imprint upon our modern secular world as well. The medical world today carries the very emblem memorializing this event; the American Medical Association, for instance, has as its emblem a serpent hanging on a pole.

As to the mere technical matter of the use of words, three different words were used in one verse in the book of Hebrews to describe certain analogies. The writer explained that an aspect of the liturgical service was simply following the design revealed to Moses which originated in heaven. Speaking of that service it is stated, ". . . who serve the **copy** (*hypodeigma*) and **shadow** (*skia*) of the heavenly things, as Moses was divinely instructed when he was about to make the tabernacle. For He (God) said, 'See that you make all things according to the **pattern** (*typos*) shown you on the mountain'" (Heb. 8:5). Hebrews 9:24 further states that the tabernacle made by Moses was a "**copy** (*anti-typos*) of the true (the one shown him from heaven)."

The Greek *Anti-typos* can obviously be translated in English as *antitype. Anti-typos* literally means *answering to the type.* This simply indicates that the antitype will correspond as the object of the type. In this regard the apostle Peter spoke of the great water baptism of judgment in Noah's day; those waters lifted up the ark wherein Noah and his family were saved. In a similar manner Peter said, "There is also an *antitype* (*antitypos*) which now saves us—baptism, not the removal of the filth of the flesh (i.e., not the typical water baptism), but the answer of a good conscience toward God . . ." (1 Peter 3:21). The antitypical baptism which cleanses the conscience is spiritual in nature and is actually mentioned earlier in context (see verse 18, which is Christ's *death baptism* for the sins of the world).

Now the apostle Paul specifically indicated that the Jewish Passover fulfills the criteria of a *typology* which points directly to fulfillment in Christ—"Christ our Passover is sacrificed for us" (1 Cor. 5:7). In addition, Paul wrote that the Law festival celebrations stood "as a *shadow* of things to come" (Col. 2:16-17). Therefore, we can be confident when we approach the subject of the Passover that we should be cautious and submissive to the Holy Spirit in order to properly and clearly understand the message. We can pray the prayer of David to the Lord "Open my eyes, that I may behold wondrous things from Your Law" (Psalm 119:18).

## Typology is also Important for Other Reasons

*First of all*, typology is one clear proof of the *Divine Inspiration* of the Scriptures. The Hebrew writers themselves accurately and faithfully wrote down what the Holy Spirit led them to say without always knowing or realizing the long range fulfillment and application of what was given. Of course we now know that the Holy Spirit Who was leading them did know of the application to the future. The *type*, therefore, sits in the story like an encrypted message awaiting fulfillment. When the time of fulfillment came, the New Testament writers also had to have Divine inspiration to read and, as it were, decode the messages. Only the same Spirit of God could enable them to see and understand the truths hidden in the original inspired accounts. The parallelisms between the original messages and their final applications are often astonishingly beautiful and clear in explaining important revelations from God. This fact reinforces the doctrine of the Divine Inspiration of the Scriptures.

*Second*, typology demonstrates the amazing *Unity* of the sacred writings. It has been pointed out in the past that the Bible was written over a period of more than 1500 years, by over 40 different writers from all walks of life, in two or more different languages, on three different continents—and yet it tells one singular story with one central character. Through the fact of Scriptural typology, both the Hebrew Scriptures and the Greek Scriptures are of necessity vitally connected and supportive of each other. The Hebrew writers were moved upon by the Spirit of God to give their accounts faithfully; it is likewise true that the writers of the Greek Scriptures were moved upon by the same Holy Spirit to give accurate illumination of the Hebrew Scriptures, thus complementing the truths and compiling all into one *unified* and *complete* revelation.

*Third*, typology in the Scriptures is often an amazing form of *Prophecy*. In the study of typology one can view the Scriptures as a grand stage upon which actors are living out what is going to happen in the future. In fact, there is often no better way to write prophecy than to act it out in the form of the lives and events of certain peoples. For instance, when we see Abraham taking His well-beloved son up to mount Moriah to sacrifice him (Gen. 22), we behold an unbelievably clear picture of the supreme sacrifice made by Almighty God of His own well-beloved Son on that very spot over seventeen hundred years later as recorded in the New Testament. Therefore, in many typologies we have laid out for us surprising details which teach God's intended purposes fulfilled in the process of time.

Now, all of this is precisely what we will be seeing when we explore aspects of the typology of the Passover celebration. We shall note that two of the important characteristics of this event were its *scheduling* for the sacrifice of the lamb and also for the special offering of the Firstfruit Wave-sheaf.

# NEWS FLASH

Just *three days* after I had signed the FORWARD to the new edition of *CHRIST OUR PASSOVER* in 2007, we heard the news over the radio that Pope Benedict XVI indicated in a homily, celebrating the traditional Thursday Mass of the Lord's Supper, that in all probability Christ actually was crucified on Thursday instead of the traditional "Good Friday." I almost fell out of my chair, so to speak. I jumped up and went into the room where the radio was and said to my wife, "Did I hear that right?—Did he say—" "Yes!" my wife said, "you heard it right!" I could hardly believe it and thought the news reporter must have made some kind of a mistake. However, it was confirmed a little later by another similar report wherein the reporter, himself, sort of joked, "Maybe now we should say 'Good Thursday' instead of 'Good Friday.'"

The next week, after Christendom's Easter celebration was over, I called two Roman Catholic organizations to see if they had any explanation for this, but as of then they knew nothing. Finally, the pope's actual homily was published by "The Wanderer." This is the oldest and most orthodox of Roman Catholic newspaper publications in the United States. And, sure enough, the present Pope Benedict XVI, who is supposed to be a scholarly pope, had publicly stated that in light of more recent discoveries of the Qumran manuscripts we can understand that the apparent contradiction in the Gospels about the actual day of Christ's death had been resolved. The pope did not use the words "a Thursday crucifixion instead of a Friday crucifixion" as the announcer had. However, what the pope said was that Christ in all probability died, according to the Gospel of John, at the actual *"hour of the sacrifice of the lambs." "This means,"* the pope explained, *"that He must have died the day before Passover (or Easter)."* And he added that this means *"He could not have personally celebrated the Paschal Supper."* What it also meant was that Christ ate the Passover a *"day earlier, without a Passover lamb."* (The emphasis here is mine, J.L.) The pope explained that he thought Christ was probably following the Qumran calendar. Of course the literal interpretation of this is what the announcer had given, that Christ must have died a *"day earlier"* on Thursday instead of the traditional Friday. I am sure there will be adjustments forthcoming by Catholic apologists concerning this.

So now I can say, with a smile on my face, that I have no less an authority for what I have concluded and written than the very head of the largest sect in Christendom, himself. In fact, the present pope claims to be the modern representative of those "church fathers" who originally chose to realign the death of Christ for commemoration. In this regard, the pope's present admission stands as a correction to those early "fathers." I have included the statements from the pope's message in Appendix J. In this immediate updated edition of the subject I have also included a quotation from the pope's latest book *Jesus of Nazareth—Holy Week* (2011), wherein he specifies in detail his conclusion as to the day upon which Christ actually died.

This year (2007) the Jewish Passover fell on our April 2-3, whereas Christendom's celebrations followed by several days. It was on the 5th of April, as the pope was celebrating a traditional Thursday Mass in commemoration of "The Lord's Supper" that he made his statements. Of course the pope made no expression about the potential bewilderment that would follow because of such a disclosure. In the year A.D. 325, at the Council of Nicaea, the so-called "church fathers" set the dates for Christ's death and resurrection and all the celebration that should follow. For the last one thousand, six hundred and eighty two years since that time Christendom has primarily been the one agent most responsible for the error and the confusion.

As a result of this latest disclosure, I think you will enjoy this particular study all the more. The conclusion that I made in this study is solidly based on a careful study of the actual Biblical facts as well as certain historical data which has been available for as long as the events themselves.

Jack W. Langford, May 4ᵗʰ, 2007


P.S. Pope Benedict XVI later recognized that the Qumran calendar had nothing whatsoever to do with the correction of the day Christ ate the Last Supper and was later tried and crucified.

# Chapter 1

# PRELIMINARIES

The Passover is properly designated in Jewish literature as "THE" holiday of Judaism. It is the first and oldest feast to be observed during the calendar year as God ordered through Moses. It has also been called *"The Festival of Redemption"* by Jewish writers because it memorializes Israel's redemption from Egyptian bondage and the redemption of all Israel's firstborn from death. Christian theology understands the Passover to be one of the most outstanding typologies illustrating the means whereby God would accomplish spiritual redemption for all humanity through the antitypical Passover Lamb—the Lord Jesus Christ. The bloodstained lintel and doorposts of the homes where the original Passover in Egypt took place point forward to the bloodstained cross through which, as it were, trusting mortals can enter by faith and be eternally protected from the wrath to come. Such obvious and beautiful parallelism demands the consensus of all who would rightfully judge that the ancient type coincides precisely with the events and benefits surrounding the death of Jesus Christ as recorded in the Greek Scriptures. One of the fruits of this study is to demonstrate, beyond any shadow of a doubt, that it does so to God's intended perfection.

# Harmony of Events

A very interesting and controversial subject, which has stymied many Bible students for centuries, has been the proper harmony of the events of Christ's suffering and death with the Passover and Feast of Unleavened Bread as it took place at the time of Christ. It was obviously God's prearranged plan that Christ's death and resurrection occur at the precise time of the annual Jewish Passover Festival. All four Gospels unite in telling us this. No serious Bible student believes that this timing was accidental. It was obviously purposed for the correlation between the type and the antitype.

Therefore, outlining an accurate and unforced chronology of the days and events as they unfolded at the time of Christ's death is important. First of all, it will enhance for us the beauty and perfection of the prophetic typology. Then, we are to remember that this great event took place at the very "climax of the ages" (Heb. 9:26). It is the focal point of all dispensational time in God's dealing with the spiritual redemption of all people (Gal. 4:4-5). Lastly, it will also expose some of modern Christendom's traditional fallacies which horribly distract from the truth of the revelation. It should be very obvious to any person reading the New Testament that nowhere in all its pages is there the slightest indication that the early Christians ever celebrated this event called "Easter." The resurrection of Christ was most certainly meant to be daily "demonstrated" in the Christians' new lives, rather than being ritually "celebrated" once a year, thank God! In fact, spiritual brethren recognize the modern ritual celebration as a distraction from the reality which God intended.

# Disruption of Harmony

The Devil has always designed confusion to cloud the beauty of events as described in the Scriptures. Today most of Christendom has, frankly speaking, adopted the totally uninspired and unauthorized celebration called "Easter." The truths of Christ's death and resurrection at the annual Jewish Passover are now surrounded by a crude mixture of elaborate papal and pagan rituals. The traditional dating of events surrounding the Easter celebrations is another primary source of the confusion that many have used to discredit the Bible.

Early "Imperial Church" theologians, in trying to pinpoint certain days to celebrate in their Easter pageantry, took a position regarding this subject that was not only quite hasty, but also very inventive. Thus, traditional Christendom inherited what was "apparent" to these early "scholars," namely, that Christ was crucified on the afternoon of Nisan 15, which was the High Sabbath of the Jewish Feast of Unleavened Bread and the day *after* the Passover. This is still the position that is traditionally held in Christendom to this day (even though Pope Benedict XVI admits the Catholic Church stands in error). They thought the crucifixion occurred on a Friday of the Roman calendar, and for some further quirk of logic, traditionalists came to call it "Good Friday." Furthermore, according to this initial supposition, the resurrection of Christ would occur only *one and a half days* later on Sunday morning, even though the Scriptures clearly say the resurrection was three days later.

Church history tells us that in very early times (A.D. 150-A.D. 250) many of the Eastern churches of Asia Minor had chosen to "celebrate" the death and resurrection of Christ on the annual Jewish Passover of Nisan 14. The Western churches (centering in Italy), on the other hand, began their "celebrations" on the Sunday after Passover. To be united they decided to formulate a singular date for the celebration and to *disassociate* it from the Jewish Passover. The Council of Nicaea (or Nice, A.D. 325) made decrees and rules for fixing the date of the whole Easter season. There is no need but to briefly mention here the complicated scenario whereby the Council reckoned the date for celebrating these events. First, it decreed that Easter would be reckoned from the occurrence of the spring equinox (the time in spring when the lengths of the day and night are equal). The church fathers calculated March 21$^{st}$ as that time (actually, it varies in occurrence). Then they stated that the next full moon which occurred after this date was to be regarded as the full moon of the "Easter Month," and the next occurring Sunday would be Christendom's celebration of Easter.

Needless to say, Christendom's "Holy Week" will vary from year to year as much as one month—anywhere from March 22nd to April 25th. Obviously, the Roman celebrations will usually not fall at the time of the Jewish Passover celebrations. This is also why Easter has come to be called "The Moving Holiday." (It most certainly was a "removal" from reality and the truth.)

You can easily see why many have challenged the traditional views of these events which have long been ordered by the Roman Catholic Church. Sad to say, most Protestants have returned to these celebrations after they broke away from them during the Reformation. Even sadder still, many Protestant theologians have worked extra hard to reinforce the traditional views of the actual day of Christ's death during that final week. This only magnifies the confusion. Infidels, Secular Humanists, Liberals and Modernists in Christendom, so-called "Higher Critics," and then Jewish writers as well have all taken their cue from the confusion and have loudly proclaimed that the *Bible contradicts itself* in accounting these events.

It is, however, necessary to acknowledge that there is an *apparent contradiction* in the New Testament texts. The three Synoptic Gospels (Matthew, Mark and Luke) plainly state that Christ ate a Passover supper with the disciples before He was betrayed to be crucified. On the other hand, the Gospel of John, in similar plain language, states that after the crucifixion of Christ a Passover supper was yet to be eaten. Infidels (including religious infidels) don't care about a solution to the apparent problem because they are only interested in ridiculing the Scriptures. In reality, conscientious Christians, who have been "regenerated by the unblemished and spotless blood of the Lamb . . . and through the living and abiding Word of God" (I Peter 1:18, 19 and 23), are not at all satisfied with pagan contamination, traditional suppositions or apparent contradictions.

## *A Positive Solution*

This is a Bible study which will offer a positive solution to the contradictory dilemma that Christendom itself has actually created. It is a harmony which is written after many years of patiently allowing the facts to be seen in their natural Biblical setting. The problem is most certainly not with the Bible, but in our preconceptions of what we think the Bible ought to be saying. I believe that the reading of this material will cause you to rejoice in the veracity and beauty of the Word of God on this subject. Indeed, this study will likewise prove that the various infidels themselves have actually fallen into a trap which will be to their own embarrassment.

It is a fact that reading through the Gospel accounts of the Passover season and the associated events as they took place in Christ's day could at first seem to be confusing, if not contradictory. Those who have more knowledge about the magnitude of the controversies in this area of Bible study may want to ask—"Mr. Langford, what makes you think you can unravel such a thorny problem which scholars have wrestled with for centuries?" My answer is simple. If the secrets of God's Word are to be unlocked on the basis of intellect, scholastic ability, personal wizardry, or mastery of ancient languages and comprehension of historical materials, then I would be the last one to approach for an answer. However, it has been my experience, as a student of the Word of God, to prayerfully and patiently study the Scriptures depending upon the guidance and illumination of the Holy Spirit Whom Christ plainly has promised to all believers for the very purpose of comprehending spiritual realities (1 Cor. 2:1-16). To claim this benefit is not spiritual arrogance; it is a simple reliance upon Christ's promised provision (John 16:13). If this has truly been my procedure and trust, then in all simplicity, I may have an advantage which some others do not have.

I do not believe for one second that I have found some long lost secret. Rather, I believe many Bible students have understood these facts throughout the ages. It has been my desire, in my own study of the Word of God, to simply obey the Scriptures in "proving all things and holding fast that which is good" (1 Thess. 5:21). I am eager to share with you the truths I have found.

## Outline of the Passover Subject

When the Children of Israel first heard Moses lay out before them God's revelation of the Passover subject, to be first enacted there in the land of Egypt, they probably never realized that they were actually hearing a clear outline plan of the supreme sacrifice of the Son of God on their behalf, to be precisely carried out some fifteen hundred years in the future. Amazing as it may seem, this is precisely what God had revealed to Moses. Consequently one, who investigates this subject of the death of Jesus Christ as it occurred in the setting of the celebration of the annual Passover, must have a comprehensive understanding of the Passover subject as revealed in the Word of God. (For the Biblical detailed references about this Feast, please read the list of Scriptures given in Appendix F at the conclusion of this study.)

To begin with, in reading the Hebrew Scriptures, one will immediately observe that the *Passover* and the *Feast of Unleavened Bread* are minutely connected, if not slightly overlapping, in the order of their occurrences. The afternoon ("evening," see Appendix A) of *Abib* 14 is called "The Lord's Passover" (Lev. 23:5) and the 15th day beginning at sunset is the first day of "The Feast of Unleavened Bread." However, the Passover supper is actually eaten on the night beginning the 15th day (Lev. 23:6) and is the first meal of that Feast of Unleavened Bread. The Feast of Unleavened Bread lasts for seven days. Because of this close connection, sometimes the whole Feast also came to be called *"Passover"* (Ezek. 45:21; Luke 22:1 and Acts 12:3, 4). (Later, from the time of the captivity in Babylon, the name of this first month was changed to *Nisan.*)

In brief, the Passover and Feast of Unleavened Bread consist of the following procedures (we are only concerned here with the major daily events)—

1.  A spotless lamb was selected (a male of the first year) on the 10th day of the first month (of the sacred year calendar) to be kept until the 14th day (Exo.12:3, 6).
2.  On the 14th day all leaven was cleansed from the homes. The lamb was to be sacrificed on the afternoon of that day. The lambs were then roasted with fire. Total preparation was made to eat the Passover meal that coming night after sunset (Exo. 12:6). (We shall later note that this day is called *"Preparation Day."*) Initially, in Egypt, the blood of the lamb was sprinkled by means of the hyssop bush, upon the door posts and lintels of their houses. This aspect of the observance was not repeated in Israel's yearly observance of the Feast.
3.  The 15th day commences with the setting of the sun (according to the Jewish calendar day reckoning) and the highlight of this night is the eating of the Passover meal along with its prayers and services (Exo. 12:8). The meal consisted of the roasted lamb, unleavened bread and bitter herbs (Exo. 12:8). (Later the customary wine was added to the meal—Lev. 23:2 and 13.)
4.  Beginning with this 15th day, unleavened bread was to be eaten for seven days (Exo. 12:15). (We will note much later in Israel's history a slight variation of this where they began eating unleavened bread even on the 14th day.)

5. The 15th day and the 21st day are regarded as special *High Sabbath Days* and no manual labor is allowed, other than preparation of foods for meals and other household chores (Exo. 12:16 and Lev. 23:7-8).

6. A final but vital aspect of this Feast is the offering of the *Sheaf bundle* (Hebrew, *Omer*—a measure) of *Firstfruits* of freshly cut grain on the morning after the first regular seventh day Sabbath which occurs during the Feast (Lev. 23:11). (Later we will note a variation in the particular Sabbath chosen for the performance of this offering in Jewish custom).

7. This bundle of freshly cut grain would be a special *Wave Offering* to God and was to stand as a token of the greater spring harvest which would be celebrated on the day after the occurrence of seven successive Sabbath days (meaning 50 days later). No new grain was to be eaten by the people of Israel until this particular *Wave Offering* of *Firstfruits* of grain had been made (Lev. 23:15-16). I will be capitalizing this special offering throughout this study to show its importance.

8. In this regard the Passover and Feast of Unleavened Bread would serve as the first of the three Feasts (Pentecost and Tabernacles being the other two) wherein all the Israelite males were required to attend the services "before the Lord" in Jerusalem (Exo. 23:14-17).

We shall see in this study that the Passover events beautifully typify the Lord Jesus Christ in His substitutionary death, burial and resurrection for all humanity. The story of redemption is spelled out by **a)** the *selection* of the Passover Lamb, **b)** the *observation* of the Passover Lamb for several days, **c)** the actual *sacrifice* of the Passover Lamb, and finally **d)** by the *Wave Offering* of the *Firstfruits* of grain several days later. Christ not only was *chosen* to be the atonement for the sins of the world, but He also was found to be *without blemish*, and He actually *died* as the antitypical Passover Lamb. Finally, He was gloriously *raised* from the dead and *ascended* up to God for our justification as typified in the routine of the Sheaf of Firstfruits being waved up in the air on Sunday morning. "Christ our Passover" also delivers the believer from the worst bondage of all, the enslavement of sin. (See the discussion on "Slavery" in Appendix H at the end of this study.)

## *Additional Preliminary Notes*

Some important notes are appropriate and must be understood before we begin. A few of these facts are of general incidental matters, whereas others can be crucial to a proper alignment in our understanding of certain statements in the Scriptures. So let us take notice of further background information that is, first of all, available to us from the Bible itself, as well as from secular historical facts.

1.  It is most important to realize that though the law concerning the celebration of the Feasts was to be meticulously followed, yet there was a certain degree of *pliability* which God allowed in their observances, as well. This is especially true as it relates to the observance of Passover. Here are examples:

    *a)* an alternate date for the observance of Passover (one month later) was stipulated in case someone was unable to partake of it at the appointed time due to some ritual uncleanness—see Numbers 9:9-12;

    *b)* on one recorded occasion there was an exception made for those who were not ceremonially clean even on the second month allowed for its observance—see 2 Chron. 30:2, 3 and 15-20;

    *c)* on this same occasion God further allowed an extended celebration of the whole Feast of Unleavened Bread for an additional seven days—see 2 Chron. 30:23; and

***d)*** according to Deut. 16:1-8, once the people of Israel came out of their wilderness journey and into the Land of Promise, they were to sacrifice a ritual Passover lamb only at the Tabernacle or Temple where God placed His Name. The observance of the Feast and the eating of unleavened bread were to continue throughout the whole land by all the households. However, only in Jerusalem could a ritual sacrifice be made. This meant that the families throughout the land and later in the dispersion, who could not attend the services at Jerusalem, would substitute for a sacrificial lamb in their eating of the Passover meal. It is customary for the Jews scattered throughout the world today to have only a shank bone of a lamb at their Passovers in order to comply with this law.

Thus I say again, there was a degree of pliability that God allowed in the historical observances of Passover. These did not contradict any of the truths reflected by the Feast day.

2.  In this same vein, it will become evident that at the time of Christ there were some other alterations in the observance of the Feast. This was some 500 years after the last recorded observance of Passover in the Hebrew Scriptures. Some modifications should not be surprising. These alterations involved some traditional changes of significance at the time Christ observed the Feast. I say again, these did not contradict any spiritual truth reflected in the Passover event but these are, however, very crucial for us to recognize if we are to arrive at a correct harmony of these events.

    For instance, you will note in the Gospel records that the 14th day of Nisan, when the lambs were sacrificed, was now called *"the first day of unleavened bread."* See—Mark 14:12—

    "Now on the first day of Unleavened Bread, when they killed the Passover lamb . . ." (See also Luke 22:7.)

In the Law, however, "the first day" of unleavened bread was the 15<sup>th</sup> day of Nisan and from that day on through the next six days unleavened bread was to be eaten (Exo. 12:8, 15, 18-20; Lev. 23:6 and Num. 28:17). Thus we can see that at the time of Christ the Gospel writers are telling us they were in the custom of beginning the days of unleavened bread a *day early*. We shall also see that several historical references, such as from Josephus, will confirm this. So to try and bring the day mentioned in the Gospel records under the exact terms of the Law without realizing these changes could cause no little confusion in attempting to differentiate or identify the days. Yet we must abide by exactly what the Gospel writers say are the facts of the case since that was, indeed, the custom at that time. No doubt at the time of Christ the Jewish people were not merely attempting to make sure that they had no leaven in their celebration on the 15<sup>th</sup> by actually starting to eat unleavened bread on the 14<sup>th</sup>, but they were actually observing the whole celebration an extra day—*in this case a day earlier.*

3.  Also at the time of Christ, another alteration was being practiced similar in nature to their eating unleavened bread a day early. That was the practice of eating a Feast meal on the beginning of the 14<sup>th</sup> day preliminary to the regular Passover meal which would be eaten at the beginning of the 15<sup>th</sup> day. The significance of this fact becomes highly important to anyone doing research on this subject. If the Jewish people now ate a pre-Passover meal on the beginning of the 14<sup>th</sup> day, the question arises—*is it possible that this was the actual meal Christ partook of with His disciples on the night of His betrayal?* He would have eaten a Passover Feast meal with His disciples before He would actually suffer at the very time the Passover lambs were sacrificed. After this, the regular Passover meal would be eaten.

### *It has been well-known that there was—*

## More Than One Passover Meal

For many years certain Bible teachers (and now Pope Benedict XVI) have strongly contended that Christ must have eaten a pre-Passover supper, or simply, He ate the Passover a day early. I believe that we will see this as Biblically correct. The Gospel writers clearly reveal that there were two different "Passover" meals in view at the time of Christ. First, the three Synoptic (similar) Gospels tell us that certain of the apostles were sent to prepare a **"Passover"** meal for Christ to eat together with them before He was to die (Matt. 26:17-19; Mark 14:12-16 and Luke 22:8-15). The Gospel of John also tells us that this last supper was actually **"before the Feast of Passover"** (John 13:1). Then with further precision John states that the next morning, after the arrest and preliminary trial of Christ, the priests would not go into the Gentile "judgment hall lest they should be defiled; so that they might **eat the Passover**" (John 18:28). In addition, John added that the day on which Christ was crucified was **"the preparation for Passover"** (John 19:14). Consequently, if these texts from all four Gospels are to be taken literally, and if they do not contradict each other, then there were *two different* Passover meals eaten at the time of Christ. There was a preliminary Passover meal eaten on the evening beginning Nisan 14 and the regular Passover meal was eaten on the evening beginning Nisan 15.

Historically speaking, there is no denying the fact that there was a *preliminary* Passover meal eaten in the custom of the Jews in Palestine at the time of Christ. This has never been a secret. Historical examples of this are the following—

1. Alfred Edersheim, in his monumental and very popular work, *The Life And Times Of Jesus The Messiah*, states in the Appendix that at the time of Christ "the **Passover,** in the popular and

canonical, though not in the Biblical, sense **began on the 14th [of] Nisan on Wednesday Evening**" (Vol. 2, page 479).

2. Edersheim further makes reference to the historian Josephus (a contemporary of early Christianity—*Antiq.* II, 15.1), who regarded the Feast to last "**eight days** (instead of 7) **beginning on the 14th**."

3. In addition, the *Jerusalem Talmud* (Jer. Pes. 27d) reckoned that the "**Pesach**" (Passover) of that time to actually begin "**on the 14th**."

4. There has also been a very thorough work done more recently to show the Jewish setting for early Christianity. The Foundation Compendia Rerum Iudaicarum ad Novum Testamentum, edited by Safrai, Stern, Flusser and Van Unnik, produced the work entitled *The Jewish People of the First Century* which states this custom. It says concerning the eve (beginning the 14th of Nisan) of the day before Passover, "The eve itself was a *sort of feast,* because the paschal sacrifice was offered that afternoon" (Volume 2, page 809, emphasis mine, J.L.). This means there was a feast meal on the evening beginning Nisan 14 which primarily celebrated the Passover sacrifice to be offered later in the afternoon of that same day.

5. Actually, this custom of beginning the Feast a day early on the 14th is still carried on to this very day by the Jews in Israel. Rabbi Riskin, chief rabbi of Efrat and dean of the Ohr Tora Institutions, has recently written in the *Jerusalem Post* (Jan. 15, 1994, in an article entitled *"Blood and Redemption"*)—

> Surprisingly enough, few people realize that here in Israel we also have an extra day [in the celebration of The Passover festival], but it arrives *before* the start of the festival, *the 14th day of Nisan.* Unfortunately, its unique feature is generally overlooked in modern times . . . The 14th day of Nisan is the one day festival of *the Passover sacrifice,* the paschal lamb (hag haPesah); the 15th day commences a seven-day festival of matzot and redemption (hag haMatzot).

6.  Rabbi Riskin further states that the celebration of the 14th day traces all the way back to the *Babylonian Talmud* (Pesahim 5a) which discusses the observance that should be had on the 14th day—"***the day before*** the seven-day festival begins." (All the **bold** emphasis above is mine, J.L.)

So it is that the historical record has been quite clear that there was a celebration of the Passover Sacrifice a day earlier than the actual Mosaic Passover. Indeed, this observance is still carried on in Israel to this modern time. Not only was this earlier Feast meal eaten on the evening beginning the 14th day done in preparation for the actual Passover sacrifice which was carried out on the close of that same 14th day, but so also were the truths that Christ brought to the attention of His disciples at the supper He ate the night of His betrayal. The unique truths that Christ expounded upon would most certainly *prepare* the apostles for a fuller comprehension of His own suffering as the antitypical Passover Lamb, to die later in the afternoon on the 14th day, exactly at the time of the sacrificing of the Passover lambs. In addition, it has always been noteworthy that there was actually no mention of Christ and the disciples eating a Passover lamb on the night of their last supper. Instead of using an actual Passover lamb to illustrate the symbolism of His death and suffering (which most certainly, it would seem, would have been done had it been there) Christ used two other available ingredients—the bread and the wine. Was part of the reason because the lambs had not yet been sacrificed?? We will allow the Scriptures to speak for themselves as we answer this question in the following pages.

It is also a well-known fact that the Jews of the dispersion, till this very day, actually eat *two* Passover meals in their observance. They eat their Passover meals (often called the *Sedar*) on the beginning of the 15th day and *repeat it* on the beginning of the 16th day as well. This came to be practiced because the Jewish calendar is primarily a lunar calendar, each month beginning with the new moon which was to be announced from Jerusalem. Jews scattered throughout the world, who could not know for certain they were eating it at the correct time, began to eat the Passover on the second day also to guarantee one of the two days would be technically accurate. In our modern age, with quick and accurate communications, this practice simply remains as a relic of a custom developed during the early centuries of the dispersion.

Needless to say, at this point it is entirely possible, from both the information of specific Biblical statements and from the above historical secular sources (both of which have generally been ignored), to understand that Christ could have made that earlier Passover meal His last Passover with His disciples before He suffered as "Our Passover" at the very time the actual Passover lambs were being sacrificed.

In light of these facts it will be very important to read the Gospel accounts very carefully to see how they fit into this setting.

## *Special Notations*

1.  As indicated earlier, the Jewish reckoning of each day is to begin at sunset and not at midnight as in our Roman calendar days. Thus, the days of the week before Christ died will always begin with the evening, and usually with the evening meal sometime after sunset.
2.  The correlation between the Jewish and Roman days is established at the point of the resurrection of Christ, which was plainly called *"the first day of the week;"* one works backward from that time. In working backwards we first note that it was the morning of the "first day of the week" (i.e., Sunday) when the tomb was found empty. The day before had to be the regular Jewish Sabbath (i.e., Saturday). In this case, the day before the regular Sabbath was the High Sabbath Day of the Feast of Unleavened Bread.

This was a Friday on the Roman calendar and Nisan 15 on the Jewish calendar. The beginning of this day on the Jewish calendar was the evening before, which was on Thursday of the Roman calendar. The evening beginning this 15th day was the time when the regular Passover supper would be eaten. When there are Scriptural statements about how many days it was "before Passover," one simply counts backward from the point of this supper.

There is generally recognized agreement by chronologists on this arrangement. The real problem which has troubled chronologists is the proper interpretation of the Scriptures as to which *day* it was that Christ ate the last supper, was betrayed, tried and crucified. Those whom I call the "*traditionalists*" believe Christ ate the regular Passover supper on the evening beginning the 15th day, and that He was therefore crucified later on the afternoon of that day, which would naturally be a Friday and a day after the Passover. However, as I will be showing and proving in this study, Christ ate the pre-Passover supper beginning the 14th day and was therefore crucified in the afternoon of that same Jewish day at the exact same time the Passover lambs were being sacrificed. This was Thursday of the Roman calendar.

3. The common use of the word "day" as used in the Gospel accounts in this situation can either simply mean the whole 24 hour time period, or just the daytime hours—such as night and day.

4. The original expression about the Passover being on "the 14th day at *evening*" (Exo.12:6) does not mean the evening that began the 14th day, but rather the evening that closed the 14th day (see Appendix A).

5. Originally, the first month of the Jewish calendar was called "Abib." This was its Hebrew name—See Exo. 12:2 and 13:4. Later, after the captivity, it was called "Nisan." This was the name given by the Babylonians. See Esther 3:7 and Neh. 2:1.

6. The term *"Passover"* can technically have different shades of meaning—

    a.) The word *Passover* is derived from the action of Jehovah who at midnight on Nisan 15 went throughout the land of Egypt to destroy the firstborn of each Egyptian household, but *"passed over"* the homes of the children of Israel where the blood of the lambs had been applied to the doorposts of their houses. Thus, this night is specifically the *"Passover"* evening and the Feast that is taken at the beginning of this night is the *"Passover"* supper.

    b.) However, since the lamb was sacrificed in the afternoon of the close or "evening" of Nisan 14 and the Passover supper was eaten shortly thereafter (at the beginning of Nisan 15), thus the designation of *"Passover"* is often tied to the close of this 14th day—see Lev. 23:5; Num. 28:16 and Exo. 12:6 (i.e., "the fourteenth day of the month at evening is the Lord's Passover" Lev.23:5).

    c.) As we have noted, at the time of Christ it also had become the custom in Israel to observe the Passover meal in a preliminary manner a day early with special emphasis upon the Passover lamb to be sacrificed at the close of that day. In this case, the whole 14th day, especially the evening meal at the beginning of this day, could also be customarily referred to as *"Passover."*

    d.) In addition, as we noted earlier, in Christ's day and until this present time, the term *"Passover"* came to be used as the designation for the whole Festival of Unleavened Bread (see Luke 22:1 and Acts 12:3-4). This was probably done in response to one of the great Kingdom prophecies of Ezekiel (45:21) which states that in the Millennium the "Passover" will be a Feast of seven days eating unleavened bread.

e.) The Passover event has been designated several ways in Judaism—

*Chag he-Aviv*, meaning The Spring festival.

*Chag ha-Matzoth*, meaning The Festival of Matzahs.

*Zoman Herateru*, meaning The Time of our Freedom.

f.) To help in this study, at this stage, I have prepared a smaller chart (see below) so that one can visually see what we are talking about. This chart only covers Nisan 14, 15 and 16.

## Small Chart

*(The shaded areas represent the nighttime hours*
*and the light areas the daytime hours)*

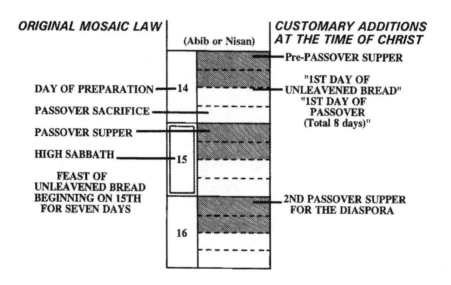

With these preliminary words we will begin
a slow and careful trek through the final week before Christ died.

# Chapter 2

# *PROGRESSION*

## *Outline of Final Week Before Christ Died*

The final week in which Christ died and the day of His resurrection are the focal points of each of the four Gospels. In addition, much of what the Gospels say in the earlier chapters is actually leading up to that climactic event of Christ's death. Of the four Gospel records, 30 chapters out of a total of 89 chapters are specifically devoted to this final week. This amounts to one-third of their combined record and shows the supreme importance of this closing week.

There are two things which I hope to demonstrate in this study. The first is the close parallel between the Passover event and the sacrifice of Jesus Christ for our sins. This is the amazing parallel between the "type" and the "antitype" in God's overall design. The second fact I want to demonstrate is the flawless perfection and consistency of the Gospel records. These records do not contradict each other as to the subject of the Passover supper or the day upon which Christ was crucified; we shall find that each stands perfectly true. Therefore, let us once again take the journey through that important time period with reverence, caution and prayer.

A general harmony shows that the writers of the four Gospels give an important and consistent countdown of days and events leading up to and immediately following the crucifixion of Christ. In Christendom this final week is called *"Holy Week"* and consists of eight days—the Sunday of Christ's triumphant entry into Jerusalem through to the following Sunday of His resurrection. However, unlike the traditionalists, who are forced to have a day unaccounted for in their chronology, we shall find that each of these days in this final week is, indeed, accounted for in the texts. In addition, I will introduce this week by the Saturday before so that we will have a total of nine days in view. I will number these days and take note of the special highlights of each one as it relates to the subject at hand.

According to the Hebrew calendar the days will be listed as Nisan 9 (Saturday) through Nisan 17 (Sunday). Please compare each of these days with those indicated on the chart on the next page of this study. The chart will indicate that the Jewish day begins at sunset and ends at the following sunset. The Roman calendar day begins at midnight and ends at the following midnight. This chart will help to give the reader a visual calendar understanding of the chronological unfolding of events and a harmony of the Gospel records. Though this study will generally harmonize the events of this calendar week, yet this is not an attempt to perfectly harmonize all the details of certain events which happened during this final week.

## NISAN 9

John 12:1, "Then *six days before the Passover,*
Jesus came to Bethany . . ."

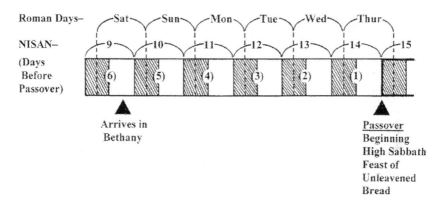

John herein uses the term *Passover* in its Mosaic and primary way, meaning the Feast meal which occurs after the close of Nisan 14 and the beginning of Nisan 15. By counting backward from the Passover (sunset between the 14th and 15th) we arrive at the 9th day of Nisan, which is *"six days before Passover."* (Note the small numerical indications just inside each day on the chart.) You will also note on the chart that this brings us to a Saturday which was the Jewish Sabbath. (As I stated earlier, one arrives at this conclusion of which Roman calendar day it was by tabulating from the resurrection day, Sunday, backwards. There is general agreement among chronologists on this procedure.)

On this ninth day before Passover Christ came to the home of Lazarus in Bethany, which is just outside Jerusalem. Because of this being a Sabbath day, some have objected to the thought of Christ and His apostles possibly traveling a distance that would violate the law of the Sabbath. Therefore, they have attempted to maneuver this arrival in a way other than as it is obviously stated. To make this maneuver is totally unnecessary. First of all the text does not tell us how far Christ traveled on that day, but simply that on that day He arrived at the home of Lazarus. However, even if this had happened, that Christ and His company had traveled a longer distance than the Law would allow on the Sabbath, the objection is easily answered by the fact that Christ's ministry required Him to do on the Sabbath what He would do any other day of the week. This is plainly demonstrated by the account of Matthew 12:1-8 where Christ and His disciples were accused of breaking the Sabbath Day. It is noteworthy in the Matthew account that Christ did not argue whether or not He had broken the technicality of the Sabbath Law. Rather, He explained *that as the priests* labored guiltlessly in the service of the temple on the Sabbath, and *as King David* was justified in eating the showbread, so it is that Christ's ministry superseded the law of the Sabbath. This explanation assumes that Christ did indeed break a technicality of the Sabbath law. Consequently, in this case of Christ arriving at the home of Lazarus on a Sabbath, we will leave this exactly as stated.

Sometime during this day, probably in the afternoon hours, Christ and the disciples arrived at the little community of Bethany which was situated on the eastern slope of Mount Olivet. This would be a relatively short distance from the Temple complex where the Feast days were celebrated. Every evening for the next three days Christ and the apostles would retire from the Temple complex to this area.

## NISAN 10

John 12:2, "There they made Him a supper . . ."

Remember again that the Jewish reckoning of the 24 hour day period always begins at sunset. Thus, this and each successive 24 hour day will begin at sunset, usually with an evening meal. We will find this to be characteristic for each of the following days. I state again for emphasis that the beginning of each day will be with the evening meal at sunset.

That evening Christ ate at the home of Lazarus whom He had raised from the dead at an earlier date (John 11:1-45). On this occasion Mary anointed the Lord's feet with very costly ointment (John 12:1-8). This text from John tells us that Judas Iscariot made the suggestion that the ointment should have been sold for money which could have been given to the poor. Though this seemed like a very pious protestation, the text tells us this was not Judas's real motivation. Christ corrected his suggestion and knew the covetousness which was really in Judas's heart. No doubt, Judas took this rebuke as a personal insult, which in his pride he deeply resented. Thus, he could have become loosened from his superficial allegiance to Jesus.

John 12:12, **"The next day** a great multitude that had come to the feast . . ."

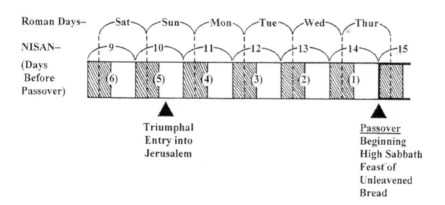

"The next day" has reference to the daylight hours of the same 10th day of Nisan. The Gospel records tell us that on this day the spectacular event of what has come to be called *The Triumphal Entry* of Christ into Jerusalem took place. (See also Mark 11:1-11.) This is our Roman calendar day of Sunday, the first day of the week. In Christendom this great event is celebrated on the Sunday before

"Easter" and is popularly called *Palm Sunday*. Rather than simply blindly following the traditional celebrations of Christendom, we are going to look at what actually highlighted this day and note its Biblical significance as it relates to the Passover subject.

## Selection of the Lamb

On this 10th day of Nisan, according to the original Law of Moses (Exo. 12:3), the Passover Lambs were to be **selected**. Every family head was to choose out a particular unblemished lamb for its Passover meal. If the family was small then the lamb could be shared by several families. On this day these lambs were to be selected and tagged, as it were, **for death.** The lambs would then be kept until the afternoon of the 14th day. Though it may be doubtful that this day was still being observed in this manner in later Jewish history, yet this is why the action of the crowds in proclaiming Jesus of Nazareth as **their choice** is so significant. While in the background the original Law had stipulated the selection of the lambs on this day, so it is in the foreground that vast crowds of people had literally become frenzied with enthusiasm in **selecting** Jesus of Nazareth as their choice. Christ's fame and popularity with the common people had increased through the few years He had ministered and performed numerous miracles and now, at this particular point in time, His popularity reached an overwhelming crescendo of enthusiasm.

Of particular significance were the words that the people began to shout—"HOSANNA ... Blessed is He that cometh in the Name of the Lord." (See the variations of this as recorded in each of the Gospel records—Matt. 21:9, 15; Mark 11:9, 10 and John 12:13). This phraseology is a quote from Psalm 118:25-26. Hosanna means **"save, we pray"** and the rest, "Blessed is He that cometh in the Name of the Lord," has reference to Jesus. Verse 21 of Psalm 118 states, *"I will praise You, for You have answered me, and have become my salvation."* There is little doubt that the crowds were looking to

Jesus as the prophesied Messiah Who would save them primarily, at this time, from the Roman oppression.

The crowds of people were so frenzied and jubilant that it made the envious and fearful religious rulers beside themselves with frustration. "Stop it! Stop it!" they were probably saying to the people. Finally these rulers even approached Jesus and appealed to Him to stop what they thought was the blasphemous enthusiasm of the multitudes. Jesus told them that if the people should stop *"the very stones would immediately cry out"* (Luke 19:40).

In frustration those clerics of old looked at each other and said, "You see that you are accomplishing nothing. Look, **the world** has gone after Him" (John 12:19). And true enough, the world had selected Him! John proceeded to tell of the Greeks who had come to the Feast and requested—*"WE WISH TO SEE JESUS!"* (verse 21). What a beautiful reminder of how John the Baptist first introduced Christ with the words, *"Behold, the Lamb of God Who takes away the sin of the **world**"* (John 1:29, 36). And furthermore, what a sober reminder of the most popular verse in the Bible—*"For God so loved **the world** that He gave His only begotten Son that whosoever believeth in Him should not perish but have everlasting life"* (John 3:16, bold and italics mine in all verses, J.L.).

And truly, this is the real significance of this day—that Christ should actually be selected as the antitypical Passover Lamb Who would guarantee the salvation of all who would place their trust in Him. Consequently, in the process of this entry into Jerusalem there was a sudden and drastic change in Christ's demeanor, and no doubt the crowd near Him was startled by it. They now listened to the words of the Man of their choice, but it would not at all be what they expected.

Suddenly, as if having been selected for **death,** Christ responded—

*The hour has come that the Son of Man should be glorified. Most assuredly, I say to you, unless a grain of wheat falls*

> *into the ground and dies, it remains alone* . . . ***NOW MY SOUL IS TROUBLED,*** *and what shall I say?* [No longer speaking to man He cries out] ***'Father, save Me from this hour? But for this purpose I came to this hour. Father, glorify Your name*** . . .' (John 12:23-33).

Almighty God, Himself, responded like "thunder" or "the voice of an Angel" some would say (verses 28 and 29)—

> *I have both glorified it, and will glorify it again.*

The nearby crowd was probably amazed as Christ went on to explain the Devil's defeat (verse 31) and also exactly how He would die (verses 32 and 33)—

> *'And I, if I am lifted up from the earth, will draw all peoples to Myself.' This he said, signifying by what **death** He would die.*

Some might very well think by the unique character of these words that Christ was somehow oblivious to the glorious reality of what was happening. It is as if He was in a different world. What would make Christ cry out like this on such a splendid occasion? Had anyone ever heard of a great ruler on the occasion of his selection by great multitudes of people suddenly turning to a morbid thought of his actual death? Here is the answer as to why it happened on this occasion! The fact is that in the background the original Law specified this day for the selection of the lambs in the first stage of the Passover observance; whereas, now in the foreground, on center stage, the antitypical Passover Lamb was selected. In actuality His selection was for DEATH. Yes! The Lord Jesus Christ knew in His soul that He was tagged for death—because He alone knew what was really happening in God's predetermined plan.

Let us never forget, though the crowd of common people deeply admired Jesus and had now selected Him openly as their potential Savior, the religious leaders stood in silent envy and hatred. They, too, had chosen Jesus of Nazareth, but for an altogether different end.

Many preachers have expounded on the sufferings of Christ, usually focusing on the crucifixion event. Others have noted that if one was to mark the actual beginning of Christ's sufferings one should look before the cross to the garden of Gethsemane where He was in awful "agony of soul" (see Luke 22:44) and "sweat, as it were, great drops of blood." But one should not stop there for the beginning of His sufferings, because such a cry was first uttered **four days earlier on this 10<sup>th</sup> day of NISAN.** This is the day He was marked for death. This is the day His deep and **awful agony of SOUL** began.

Yes, we also, as we read of these events which occurred on this day, are like the crowds of people who actually witnessed them. We are momentarily left in stunned amazement at the seeming contradiction of thought. We are thrust from great rejoicing to sudden, horribly unexplainable gloom. Yet now, from our perspective in time, we look in further amazement at the absolute precision of the Divine arrangement between the *Type* and the *Antitype. This is the day The Lamb was selected.* May God help us to more wisely praise His Holy Name and stand in awe of Him. The absolute precision of God's time clock should erase from our minds any suggestion of mere accidents or generalities in fulfillment.

# Observation of The Lamb

## NISAN 11

Mark 11:11b-18, ". . . as the hour was already late, He went
out unto Bethany with the twelve. Now the next day . . ."

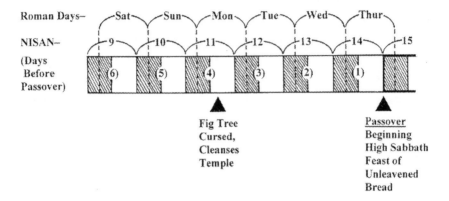

As the evening came Christ returned to Bethany to stay there that
night. This began the 11th day of Nisan. In the morning (this would
be our Monday), on His way back into Jerusalem, Christ paused at a
fig tree for an important lesson to the disciples who were with Him.
On this occasion Christ placed a curse on the fig tree because it had
no fruit. In the Scriptures the fig tree was emblematic of the nation of
Israel which had every opportunity to bear spiritual fruit in response
to the ministry of John the Baptist and Christ, Himself. However,
the nation as a whole was not responsive and would eventually be left
to a sad fate; it would be placed under a curse.

Once in the Temple Christ violently cleansed it of the business
hawkers and drew further hatred from the religious rulers who were
already planning His imminent death if at all possible (see John
11:57). Remember this was Monday on the Roman calendar. Toward
evening Christ again left the city to return to a place in Bethany.

Christ would face His first examination before the religious leaders the next day because of His action of cleansing the Temple. They asked, "Who gave You this authority?" (Mark 11:27-33). And as you read His answer, you can see that their mouths were stopped!

## NISAN 12

Mark 11:19 and 20, "When evening had come, He went out of the city. Now in the morning . . ."

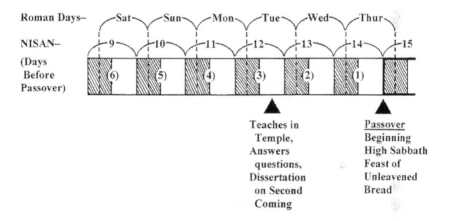

Christ once again returned to Jerusalem after having spent the night outside the city. He passed the same fig tree and completed the lesson to the disciples. They noticed how quickly the fig tree had died and even dried out. This is the 12th day of Nisan and the daylight hours will be Tuesday of the Roman calendar.

The Gospels recorded many things Christ taught on this day. Mark 11:27-12:37 and Matthew 21:17-25:46 and Luke chapters 20 and 21 record for us the long dissertations given in the Temple and the many contentions of the rulers in attempts to trap Christ in His words and thus have grounds for His death. Needless to say, they were unsuccessful. It is as if Christ, as the antitypical Passover Lamb, was subjected to the most careful scrutiny ever given to any man. This is illustrated in Matthew 22:15-22. Here is recorded the question by the Pharisees of whether or not it was lawful to pay taxes to Caesar. After silencing the Pharisees, next the Sadducees asked Him the tricky question about the resurrection, Matt. 22:23-33. After He silenced the Sadducees, the lawyer tested Him, Matt. 22:34-40. After they were all stopped, Christ questioned them as to how King David could call his distant Son (the Messiah) *"Lord"* (Matt. 22:41-46). Of course, they could not answer. There was no way they could "entangle Him in His talk" (Matt. 22:15). And after all was said and done, He was found impeccable and truly ***unblemished.*** Therefore, the only real ground for Christ's death was as the innocent substitute—the perfect Passover Lamb.

These passages go on to tell what Christ said at the close of that day, as He was once again leaving the city. He spoke of the climactic events at the end of the age, of His second coming and the great Day of the Lord.

## *Important Alignment*

One final thing which Christ told the apostles at the close of this day will help us to align ourselves and to double-check our position as to precisely where we are in the chronology of these events. This is recorded for us in Matthew 26:1-5 and Mark 14:1-2. Likewise, in these passages there is the statement concerning the aim of the rulers of the people at this point in the drama. I will emphasize this passage in bold—

> . . . after *two days* is the Passover, and the Son of Man will be delivered up to be crucified . . . Not during the Feast, lest there be an uproar among the people.

(Note again the chart on the previous page.)

By looking on the chart one can see that we are right on schedule in our understanding of the unfolding of these events. Nisan 12 is ending and just two days (Nisan 13 and 14) are left before the actual Passover and the Feast of Unleavened Bread beginning on the High Sabbath of Nisan 15. To this very time in Jewish reckoning, Nisan 14 is still referred to as "the day before Pessah [Passover]" (see *Jerusalem Post*, April 6, 1996 under "*True Freedom*" by Rabbi Riskin). Thus "two days before" includes Nisan 13 and Nisan 14.

The planners of Christ's death are fearful of the multitudes of people rioting were the death of Christ to occur on the High Sabbath Feast Day of Nisan 15. Therefore, if they are going to have Jesus killed, they are pressed to do so as soon as possible! Due to the compressed time schedule, they must act quickly. It all must be accomplished within **two days.** How can they do it? Who will help them? Nisan 13 is rapidly upon them and then the "Preparation Day" of Nisan 14—and that is all!

First of all, these religious clerics, in their unbelief and rejection of Jesus, are totally ignorant that Almighty God is arranging the schedule and they are only tools of His to reflect, by their own minds and secret councils, the execution of His plans according to His Divine schedule.

As to the chronology of events we have seen that, according to the four Gospels, there has been no gap in the day-by-day reckoning of events. We have traveled from Nisan 9 up through Nisan 12 as we have moved through the Gospel accounts. Now we are approaching the final day before Christ will be betrayed.

# *Betrayal of the Lamb*

## NISAN 13

Mark 14:3-11; Matt. 26:6-16 and Luke 22:1-6,
"And being in Bethany in the house of Simon
the leper, as He sat at the table . . ."

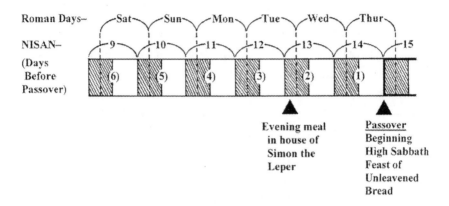

Christ returned to Bethany for this night and ate supper in the home of Simon the leper. This began Nisan 13. The daylight hours were our Wednesday. Surprisingly enough, there is general agreement among most chronologists on this schedule. At this meal a woman poured precious ointment upon the head of Christ. Christ explained that this notable deed was actually done for His burial and would be remembered throughout the ages. Thus He indicated that the time of His death was very near. There were some who criticized what they thought was a waste of the money used for this precious ointment. However, once again Christ reminded them that what she had done was honorable and that she had actually prepared His body for burial. Then Christ said that the thing she had done would be preached to the whole world as a memorial to her (Mark 14:9).

In all probability Judas remembered Christ's rebuke delivered to him a few days earlier (John 12:4-8). The very next thing the text said is that sometime during this 24 hour time period Judas found his way to the chief priests to betray Christ (Mark 14:10). Most certainly, for himself, Judas will have only the miserable "memorial" of the eternal reminder of his wicked deed.

Behind the scenes the religious leaders have taken final counsel to put Christ to death. Actually, their intent was no secret. Even the apostles had known for a long time that these leaders were seeking to kill Him (John 5:18; 7:1, 19, 25; 8:37, 40). Judas, himself, knew this as well; therefore, he must act quickly if he is to take advantage of the opportunity. Thus it is that sometime during this day (either in the late evening hours or sometime in the morning hours) Judas went into the city of Jerusalem and made contact with those who were seeking to silence this Jesus of Nazareth.

It is noteworthy that, while Judas was contracting for Christ's betrayal, Christ Himself remained outside the city of Jerusalem on this Wednesday. The negotiations between Judas and the clergy are self-evident. The religious leaders were very happy for this opportunity. Yes, it even seemed to them that providence was on their side. No doubt, the deadline was explained to Judas, *"NOT on the High Sabbath of the Feast lest there be a riot among the observers of the Feast"* (Matt. 26:5 and Mark 14:1-2). Christ will have to be relatively alone, not surrounded by crowds. Then He will be taken privately into their custody. They can hastily arrange a judgment council for His condemnation and then, "We will take care of the rest," they would say. One can easily sense the tenseness of the oncoming hours.

Judas probably returned to where Christ lodged and remained alert for a convenient opportunity. If the schedule of the religious rulers was to be complied with—and there is absolutely no Scriptural explanation to the effect that it was not—then this would be the last time Jesus would enter Jerusalem. Seemingly, like a trap, the device was set and ready to snap shut.

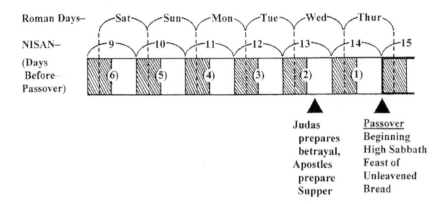

If there is no blank space in the daily accounting by the Gospel writers, then it is in the late afternoon of Wednesday (Nisan 13) that Christ sent certain disciples ahead into the city of Jerusalem to make preparations for an evening meal within the city. On this coming evening, which would be the beginning of Nisan 14, Christ would be eating with His disciples in the city of Jerusalem itself. This would be His last meal with them before His death. This, of course, is the approach of our Wednesday evening.

Let us also remember that this is the "Wednesday evening" Alfred Edersheim indicated as the historical time of the first celebration of "the Passover" on the "14th of Nisan" at the time of Christ. The Jewish historian of the first century, Josephus, said the Passover of that time was of "eight days beginning on the 14th." *The Jerusalem Talmud* (Jer. Pes. 27d) said the same thing. *The Babylonian Talmud* (Pesahim 5a) made the same observation. The work entitled *The Jewish people of the First Century* by The Foundation Compendia Rerum Iudaicarum ad Novum Testamentum also makes the very same observation. Finally, Rabbi Riskin of modern times states this custom in the *Jerusalem Post* articles.

Consequently, if there are no missing days, then this was the Wednesday evening beginning the 14th day of Nisan on which Christ and His disciples would be celebrating a Passover supper which *anticipated* the sacrifice of the Passover Lamb.

## The Famous "Missing Day"

The traditional idea of this week's chronology originated with the theologians of the *Imperial Church* in the early fourth century. They concluded that Christ's Last Supper, trial and crucifixion actually occurred on the High Sabbath of Passover of Nisan 15. Since the traditional idea of this event moves the crucifixion forward to Friday, the 15th of Nisan, whatever happened between Wednesday and Friday in this final week was naturally and unavoidably left out of the Biblical record—if their traditional view is correct. Indeed, those interpreters who follow the traditional schedule all refer to Nisan 14 as "the Missing Day," or "the Blank Day" in the Gospel records.

At the very same time everyone seems to admit that this *blank time period*, from the daylight hours of Wednesday until sunset on Thursday, appears to be highly unusual in light of how carefully the Gospels cover this final week before Christ died. That one Gospel writer might pass over this time period would not be unusual, but that all four Gospel writers leave such a blank space seems to be uncharacteristic. Of course, we need to remember that Christendom's tradition created this problem in the first place. It follows that one presumptuous error creates other irregularities. In this case we are going to find that Christendom's error has created a whole lot of confusing irregularities, not only to the whole Gospel record, but also to well-known Jewish traditions as to how and when the Sanhedrin can meet and issue a judgment. Such an event by the Sanhedrin was never to be done on a High Sabbath day such as Nisan 15.

However, if there is actually no break in the Gospel record of this most important week, then all the Gospels will account for the 14th day of Nisan—which, in fact, they do! Nisan 14 was well-known as the *"Preparation Day"* for the Passover. And indeed, all four Gospels state clearly and emphatically that this is the day upon which Christ was crucified.

*We are going to jump ahead for a moment* and survey the statements which identify the day upon which Christ was crucified. In so doing we will find that—

## The "Missing Day" is NOT MISSING!

1.  Concerning the early morning hours of this day we read from John 19:13 and 14 the following—

    > When Pilate therefore heard that saying, he brought Jesus out and sat down in the judgment seat in a place that is called The Pavement, but in Hebrew, Gabbatha. Now it was the *Preparation Day of the Passover*, and about the sixth hour. And he said to the Jews, 'Behold your King!'

    Concerning the late afternoon hours we also read from John 19: 31—

    > Therefore, because it was the *Preparation Day*, that the bodies should not remain on the cross on the Sabbath (*for that Sabbath was a High Day* [meaning the High Sabbath of Passover, Nisan 15]), the Jews asked Pilate that their legs might be broken, and that they might be taken away.

Consequently, we are to understand that according to the Gospel of John, from the early morning hours till evening, these were the daylight hours of *the Preparation Day* for the High Sabbath of the Jewish Passover. That also automatically meant Nisan 14 is in view by

John. Under no circumstance was the High Sabbath of the 15th day of Nisan ever called *the Preparation Day*. To make that holy day the *Preparation Day* would violate its holiness. If two Sabbaths followed in succession, such as the High Sabbath followed by a regular Sabbath, then the day before both Sabbaths was *the Preparation Day*. Such is the case at the time of Christ's death.

Normally crucifixion lasted for several days. In this case, since the next day was the High Sabbath of Passover (Nisan 15), the Jews asked that the death of those crucified might be hastened so that they would not be left hanging on that holy day. Again, this obviously means that the *"Preparation Day"* spoken of was the 14th day of Nisan when Christ was crucified. This is clearly stated twice in the Gospel of John so there is no mistaking what is meant. Most all critics and students of this subject admit there is no mistaking what John meant. John meant that Christ was crucified on Nisan 14 before the High Sabbath of Passover. Let us now see what the rest of the Gospel writers say—

2. Mark 15:42, 43—

> Now when evening had come, because it was the *Preparation Day*, that is, the day before the Sabbath, Joseph of Arimathea . . . asked for the body of Jesus.

Obviously Mark is in *full agreement* with John. Christ was crucified on the *Preparation Day*. This day is followed by the Sabbath. This would, of course, be the same Sabbath which John was talking about—the High Sabbath of Passover—Nisan 15.

3. Luke 23:54 Concerning the crucifixion of Christ, Luke states,

> That day was the *Preparation (day)*, and the Sabbath drew near.

This is in full accord with Mark's account, which was in full accord with John's account. The same *Preparation Day* is mentioned followed by the same (High) Sabbath. So far, the records of Mark, Luke and John are in perfect agreement.

Matthew 27:62—

> On the next day, which followed the *Day of Preparation* [that is, on the day after the crucifixion of Christ], the chief priests and Pharisees gathered together to Pilate, [to ask for guards to be placed at the tomb].

So all four Gospels are in perfect accord as to which day it was upon which Christ was crucified and died—the *Preparation Day* (Nisan 14)—and it is followed by the High Sabbath of Nisan 15. We have a very clear illustration of this recorded for us in the Hebrew Scriptures. In 2 Chronicles chapter 35, where King Josiah celebrated the Passover, we have the "fourteenth day" specified (35:1). And then, five times the words "prepare" or "preparations" are used (verses 4, 6, 14 twice and 15), and once "the service was prepared" (verse 10) is used to describe the activity of that day. In addition, it is stated that the Passover sacrifices were made on this day (verse 11). Not only does this settle the matter as to the day on which Christ was crucified, but it does away with the idea of a "Missing Day."

Some have suggested that Preparation Day in this case was simply the preparation for the regular Saturday Sabbath day. The Gospel of John answers that by clearly identifying the Sabbath as the Passover "High Day." Others have suggested that on this occasion in history both these types of Sabbath days fell upon the same day. Actually on this occasion, they fell in succession. The High Sabbath of Passover was followed by the regular weekly Sabbath. Most chronologists are in agreement with this. In addition, in the Gospel records the term *Preparation Day* takes on a special significance. Historically, Nisan 14 was generally called *"the Preparation Day"* for the Passover of Nisan 15. Though it is true that preparation is generally made on Fridays for the regular weekly Sabbaths to follow, yet those days did not have that special designation as *"the Preparation Day."* I will have more to say about this later.

## The Gospels Harmonize

As we have seen by the above quotations, all four Gospels are in perfect harmony as to the day upon which Christ died. They all identify the time of Christ's death as taking place on *"the Preparation Day,"* in particular, the day before the Passover. Most all critics of the Bible forget that all four Gospel writers say the very same thing in this regard. The clamor from the infidels and liberal Christian theologians that the four Gospels contradict themselves on this subject is actually only a reflection upon their own ignorance. This will be demonstrated over and over again throughout this study. What appears to be a factual contradiction or lack of harmony is actually not true at all.

We will find this to be the truth exemplified again in another case immediately before us. This will concern those verses from the four Gospels which introduce this day of Nisan 14. We will find that when the Gospel accounts are read from a proper perspective, any apparent disharmony or contradictions will be alleviated.

The proof of this will follow.

# Chapter 3
# PREPARATION

## The Preparation Day

There are two problems which must be solved as one approaches the texts which introduce the next day to us. First, one wants to properly identify once again exactly the day being referred to by the texts. This we have already done in a preliminary manner in the last chapter. Secondly, and of utmost importance, one must get the right perspective as to where we are in relation to that day. In other words, in positioning ourselves in reading the text are we to understand that we are at the beginning of that day, or are we at its conclusion? This we will do as we move along.

As we noted the previous passages from the four Gospels which identify the day upon which Christ was crucified, so now we want to go back and look at those passages which *introduce* this day to us. Herein is where the first mistake is made by those I call the *traditionalists*. Most of them wrongly interpret what the Gospel writers are saying about this day. And I must say it is easy to do this if we are hasty in forming conclusions. I made the mistake myself when I first studied this subject. It took me some time to get properly oriented in reading the texts. The first one is that of Matthew. It probably is the easiest one to misunderstand.

1. Matthew 26:17—

> Now on the first *day of the Feast* of Unleavened Bread the disciples came to Jesus, saying to Him, 'Where do You want us to prepare for You to eat the Passover?'

The first impression one may have in reading this verse is to think this must be talking about the "first day" of the Mosaic "Feast of Unleavened Bread" which would be Nisan15 on the Jewish calendar. If this is the case, then the Passover lambs would have already been sacrificed, and they would be ready to sit down and eat the regular Passover meal on the evening beginning the 15th day.

However, there are a few warning signs before anyone should make such a firm conclusion. First, we should note that the words *"day of the Feast"* are in italicized print which tells us these words have been added by the translators. Sometimes this is helpful and sometimes it is not. If we understand *"the Feast* of Unleavened bread" to mean the actual Mosaic Feast then indeed it would be Nisan 15 when that Feast actually began (Exo. 12:16 and 17). However, if we took the words *"day of the Feast"* out of the text, it may be simply saying "the first of Unleavened Bread," but not necessarily the first day of *"the Feast"* as spelled out by Moses. Most certainly we need to look at what the other Gospel writers say and compare all of them together.

2. Now let us turn to Mark 14:12 which makes nearly the same statement, yet adds some clarification—

> Now on the first day of Unleavened Bread, when they killed the Passover lamb, His disciples said to Him, 'Where do You want us to go and prepare, that You may eat the Passover?'

Here there are no italicized words. It is simply the first day of Unleavened Bread, but not the first day of the Feast. In added clarification, Mark tells us this is the day when "they killed the Passover lamb." Now the day the Passover lamb is sacrificed is clearly the 14th day of Nisan, and not the 15th. No doubt, Mark and Matthew are saying the very same thing, but in either case they are NOT saying this is the 15th day of Nisan, the High Sabbath Feast day.

3.  Luke 22:7 will tell us the very same thing as does Mark—

> Then came the Day of Unleavened Bread, when the Passover (lamb) must be killed.

This is confirmation to what we found in Mark. The day in view is the day when the Passover lambs were to be sacrificed. That is Nisan14 and the day *before* the regular Passover Feast takes place. These two verses correct our faulty assumption from a first reading of Matthew's account.

4.  The Gospel of John establishes this conclusion beyond doubt. John 13:1—

> Now **before the Feast of the Passover,** when Jesus knew that His hour had come that He should depart from this world to the Father . . .

I can assure you, the only reason that many interpreters do not take this passage at face value is because it devastates the *traditionalists'* view. However, in taking this passage literally, there is perfect harmony with Mark and Luke. Since this is "before the Feast of the Passover" and not the Passover itself, we would understand that this meal is the new customary pre-Passover meal which was eaten at the time of Christ, and actually is still eaten to this very day in Israel. So,

*Jack W. Langford*

once again, it is clear that this day is Nisan 14. Actually, Matthew, Mark, Luke and John are all saying the very same thing—namely, that the day has come when the Passover lambs must be sacrificed, which is the 14th of Nisan, and Christ wants to eat a special meal with His disciples at the beginning of this day. Herein, John proceeds to talk about all that Christ said during that final meal with His disciples.

## The Proper Perspective on that day

Even those who recognize that these verses are talking about the Preparation Day of Nisan 14, nevertheless view some of these verses as saying this day has just *ended* and we are about to begin the 15th day of Nisan. However, this is not the right perspective! It is very important to get the correct perspective on the verses we have just read. Let us examine the passages carefully. For instance Mark 14:12 says—

> Now on the first day of Unleavened Bread, when they killed the Passover *lamb*, His disciples said to Him, 'Where do you want us to go and prepare, that you may eat the Passover?'

Some traditionalists think this passage is saying, "the day when they killed the Passover *is past*, and they are to prepare for the next day which would be the beginning of Nisan 15." However, this is not at all what Mark is saying! Mark is actually giving the *introduction* to the day upon which they killed the Passover lambs. What he is saying is that the day has finally arrived, and this is the approach to this day when the Passover lambs would be killed. The Gospel of Luke makes this very clear—

**Then came** (not passed) the Day of Unleavened Bread, when the Passover (lamb) must be killed (Luke 22:7).

This certainly demonstrates the proper perspective in looking at these passages. In addition, remember that later in the next chapter of Mark is the verse that takes us all the way to the *end* of this day when the Passover lambs were killed. Mark 15:42—

Now when evening had come [that is, the close of this day which had been introduced in verse 12], because it was the Preparation Day, that is, the day before the (High) Sabbath . . .

Consequently, Mark 14:12 could not possibly be talking about the end of the Preparation Day, but rather its beginning. This of course proves that Matthew 26:17 and Mark 14:12 must be viewed as the introduction to this same day. Notice, therefore, how I have arranged the following verses to indicate the beginning of this very important day—as had been said—"*The most important day in the history of the world.*"

## Returning to the Schedule

We have concluded our discussion of Wednesday the 13th day of Nisan. The evening beginning that day Christ spent in the home of Simon the leper. Sometime in the late evening or the coming daylight hours Judas Iscariot made his contract with the religious rulers to betray Christ. In the afternoon of that same day Christ would send some of the disciples into Jerusalem to make preparations for eating the special Passover meal which was traditional at that time, and still is to this very day. As Rabbi Reskin says "Unfortunately, its unique feature is generally overlooked in modern times . . ."

## NISAN 14

(a) Luke 22:7, "Then came the Day of Unleavened Bread, when the Passover [lamb] must be killed."

(b) Mark 14:12, "His disciples said to Him, 'Where do You want us to go and prepare, that You may eat the Passover?'"

(c) Matthew 26:17 "When evening had come, He sat down [at the meal] with the twelve."

(d) John 13:1-2 "Now before the Feast of Passover, when Jesus knew that His hour had come . . . And supper being ended . . ."

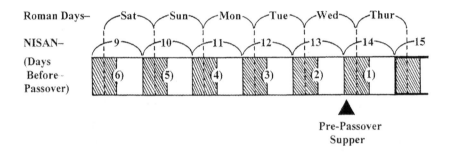

These passages, in consistency with all the foregoing facts and in the continuity of the daily accounting of this last week, must **begin** the 14th day of Nisan. Christ gave the instructions for preparing the evening meal (the customary pre-Passover supper). Christ gave many truths to the apostles during this last supper. After retiring to Gethsemane, later that night He was betrayed. A late night trial was held by the religious leaders in order to expedite their need to have Christ put to death prior to the High Sabbath. In addition, such a trial by the Sanhedrin is then allowable, whereas it would not be if it was on the High Sabbath of Nisan 15. The next morning (the daylight hours of Nisan 14) He was transferred to Pilate's and Herod's courts. His death was arranged to take place at the same time two criminals were scheduled to die—and one could be sure that these criminals were not *scheduled to die on the High Sabbath of Nisan 15*. His crucifixion would, of course, bring about His death at the very same time the Passover lambs were being sacrificed in the Temple ritual. This is Thursday on the Roman calendar. This fact will consistently be brought out, and proven beyond any shadow of doubt, as we continue to move through the Gospel accounts.

## *Errors of the Traditionalists*

Just here I want to comment on some of the obvious mistakes the early theologians made when they set the dates for the "Easter" customs. A hasty reading of the Gospel accounts, with a predisposition to prove the traditional view, would make misunderstandings inevitable.

**First,** the traditionalists read the three Synoptic Gospels where it is stated that Christ "ate the Passover with His disciples." Naturally, if one was to focus only on these statements, the first impression would be the Mosaic Passover meal which occurred on the evening beginning Nisan 15. However, careful Bible students should never solidify their conclusions until all the facts have been analyzed. One must also focus on the whole context of these events before he forms his conclusion. As I stated earlier, the Gospels indicate that there are *two* different "Passover" meals to be eaten—one that Christ ate with His disciples—and one that the religious rulers were to eat the next day. In addition, there are *many historical references* to show that, indeed, two Passover meals were celebrated in the times of Christ in Palestine. Consequently, at this juncture one must ask which Passover meal is this talking about—the pre-Passover supper—or the actual Mosaic Passover supper?

**Second,** many traditionalists realize that the passages I have just quoted (Lk. 22:7; Mk. 14:12 and Matt. 26:17) are talking about the

14<sup>th</sup> day of Nisan because that is clearly when the Passover lambs were sacrificed. But, because they think that the regular Passover supper is in view, they are forced to view these statements as being made from the perspective of the *close* of the 14<sup>th</sup> day rather than from the perspective of the *beginning* of that day. In other words, they are thinking, "then came—**AND PASSED**—the Day of Unleavened Bread, when the Passover must be killed" (Lk. 22:7). They understand these statements as saying that Nisan 14 is about over and now Christ wants to prepare for the regular Passover meal beginning on Nisan 15.

Of course, this is totally out of perspective. Nisan 14, like all other days before it, will *BEGIN* with the evening meal. Luke's account makes it clear that the 14<sup>th</sup> day *"CAME,"* not that it *PASSED!* What follows in each of the Gospel accounts is simply a full accounting of all that took place on that particular 14<sup>th</sup> day of Nisan—beginning with the evening meal.

In addition, we have seen that all four Gospel accounts agree that Christ was crucified on *"the Preparation Day"*—Matt. 27:62; Mark 15:42; Luke 23:54 and John 19:42. In addition, we have seen further evidence from 2 Chron. 35 that the "Preparation Day" was clearly "the fourteenth day of the first month (Nisan)," in preparation for Passover. If Christ was crucified on "Preparation day" then the "last supper" had to have been the supper which took place on the evening beginning Nisan 14.

Thus, each of the statements in the Gospel accounts should normally and consistently be viewed from the perspective of the *beginning introduction* to the 14th day instead of from the perspective of the end of that day. With that in mind, there will be perfect harmony with the Gospel of John which many have claimed to be contradictory to the Synoptic Gospels.

## Several Glaring Inconsistencies

These mistakes by those I call the *traditionalists* create several tremendous problems.

The first of these is that they have admittedly created a totally "blank day." From the afternoon of the 13th to the afternoon of the 14th, when the Passover lambs were sacrificed, has been called by chronologists, *The Missing Day*. By pushing Christ's death over to Nisan 15 they have opened up a one day gap in the record. Whatever takes place from Wednesday afternoon through all of Thursday is simply left out of the Biblical record in their thinking. They have also referred to this as the "blank day" in the final week of Christ's suffering. In light of this week being the primary focal point of the Gospel records, and in light of a revealed continuity about all other days, a "blank" in the record is highly improbable. As we continue through this study we will see that all the days in this important time frame are accounted for.

Second, if there is such a blank in the record and Christ was, indeed, crucified on the High Sabbath of the 15th day of Nisan, then there is absolutely NO EXPLANATION given as to why the religious rulers would go against their own judgment to do such a thing. The Gospels are clear! That was the one thing the rulers didn't want to do because it would cause a riot and they all would be in danger of being hurt. And yet, the *traditionalists* have them do such a thing and NOT A WORD is said about it. This is AMAZING! Perhaps the religious rulers today would be foolish enough to do such a thing but, most certainly, the rulers back there would never do so. Undoubtedly, the reason there is no Biblical explanation given as to why they would go against their own better judgment and counsel is because—in fact, **they didn't.**

Third, not only would the religious leaders NOT do such a thing, it is even more UNLIKELY that the secular rulers would do such a thing. They did not want a riot anymore than the clerics did. Pilate would not chance such an offense to the Jewish people. Herod was probably as brutal as Pilate. Just a few years later Acts 12:3 and 4 tell us that Herod kept Peter in prison until after the Passover and would have him killed then. If Herod would wait until after the Passover to have a disciple of Christ killed, it is obvious that Pilate would not have the Messiah, Himself, killed on the regular Passover High Sabbath Day.

Fourth, this assumption has also forced the religious rulers to call for a trial on Passover evening—the High Sabbath of Nisan 15. Jewish scholars have for centuries called this an *impossibility*. The Jewish Oxford scholar, Geza Vermes, has recently stated that he "flatly rejects as unthinkable according to Jewish Law" the notion of Jesus being tried by the Sanhedrin on Passover evening. Because of Christendom's insistence that this did happen on that night, Vermes charges that the New Testament account must be "a deplorable caricature" of unreliable history (*The Passion*, by Geza Vermes). Of course, the truth of the matter is that the Gospel writers are careful to NOT say this. There was such a trial, but it was held the night of the Preparation Day in full compliance with Jewish law. The *traditionalists*, not the Gospel records, have created this confusion.

Fifth, this assumption by the *traditionalists* forces a congestion in the time duration, from the death of Christ until His resurrection, to be that of only two days instead of the revealed "three." This is by far the most problematic and controversial factor they have created.

If we recognize that there is no break in the chronological recording of these events, there will be harmony of the Gospel records. The account will run smoothly, filling every day in this important time frame. It will also avoid the inescapable enigma of Christ being dead for only two days instead of the Scriptural "three." That Christ was raised from the dead on Sunday morning, there is no doubt. **That Christ died on Friday afternoon has been contested ever since this blunder was first made.**

### Further Testimony that Establishes the Accounting of the 14th Day of Nisan as the Day upon which Christ was Crucified

The Gospel writers give an orderly account of the whole of Nisan 14. As all the other days in this week began with an evening meal, so it is true of this day. This day began by Christ eating His last "Passover" supper with the disciples. He was betrayed about midnight, tried by the high priests in the late night hours, was judged by Pilate and Herod in the morning, and was crucified to die later in the afternoon hours. Finally, His body was taken down from the tree and buried just before sunset. Many references will further testify to the fact that this was Thursday, Nisan 14. We will take these references in somewhat of a chronological order.

1.  **JOHN 13:1** As indicated earlier, this passage plainly states that Christ's last supper with His disciples was **"BEFORE** the Feast of Passover."** There is really no need to try and explain away the face value of this clear statement as many have tried to do. In fact there is no satisfactory explanation of this passage by the *traditionalists.* If the last supper Christ ate with His disciples was the Mosaic Passover supper, then there is no other "Passover Supper" in the future—this is it! Therefore, many will say that this statement merely indicates that the moment is just "before" the eating of the Passover meal that night. The problem with this is that verse two of the passage states that the "supper" was already in progress, **"taking place"** (literal translation). Thus, the setting for this passage is not before they ate, but rather later in the progress of the meal as Judas Iscariot contemplates leaving.

The next verse indicates this. This is why some translations render verse two "and supper being ended" (K.J.V.).

2. **LUKE 22:7, 15** "Then came the day when **the Passover must be killed** [i.e., the beginning of the 14th day of Nisan had arrived] . . . I desire to eat this Passover with you **BEFORE I suffer.**" As we saw above, John 13:1 said that Christ ate this meal "BEFORE . . . PASSOVER (the Mosaic Passover)." Now Luke recorded the words of Christ that this meal was also "BEFORE I SUFFER." Since they both are referring to the same identical time period (when the Passover lambs would be killed), then we conclude that Christ actually died at the time that the Passover lambs were being sacrificed.

   In addition, the Gospel of John makes it plain that Christ's sacrifice, wherein none of His bones were broken (even though the Roman soldiers had intended to do so), was in fulfillment of the typology of the Passover sacrifice. John quoted directly from the Passover Law (Exodus 12:46 and Numbers 9:12) to the effect that not a bone of the Passover lamb was to be broken. *"For these things were done, that the Scripture should be fulfilled, 'A bone of Him shall not be broken'"* (John 19:36). Thus the full meaning of the Passover sacrifice points perfectly to the fulfilling Sacrifice of Christ both by its manner and timing.

3. **1 CORINTHIANS 5:7** "CHRIST OUR PASSOVER is sacrificed for us." This passage by the divinely inspired apostle Paul clearly *superimposes* Christ's sacrifice upon the sacrifice of the Passover lambs. Not only is the beauty of this fact inescapable, but the perfection of the timing is also inescapable.

4. **JOHN 13:29** This passage indicates that Judas Iscariot, who left the supper in order to betray Christ, could have gone out to *"buy things needed for the feast."* This, of course, would have been a total impossibility were they eating the regular Passover meal on the High Sabbath of Nisan 15. All purchases for that Feast meal had to be done on the Preparation Day of Nisan 14. Therefore, it is perfectly logical and permissible that Judas could have gone out

to purchase things on the evening of Nisan 14. This proves the fact that they were on the evening beginning Nisan 14.

5. **JOHN 18:28** In the early morning hours of that day the religious leaders had turned Christ over to the Roman authority. At this time it was stated that the Jewish leaders could not go into the Roman judgment hall but had to stay outside so that they could remain "purified in order to eat the Passover." This purification was required by the Law of Moses (Num. 9:6-10 and John 11:55) in order to participate in the Passover meal and its services. Thus, the regular Passover feast had not yet taken place.

6. **JOHN 18:39** This passage records the fact (noted by the other Gospel writers as well) that Pontius Pilate customarily released a prisoner *"at the Passover."* This use of the term "Passover," as we have stated earlier, has reference to the afternoon of Nisan 14 when they slaughtered the Passover lambs (Lev. 23:5; Num. 28:16-17 and Exo. 12:6). This was the *Preparation Day* for the Passover itself. Thus it was on this day that Pilate, in order to generate friendship with the Jewish people, made such a friendly gesture.

Of course, at this time Pilate left it up to the crowds (who were prompted by the religious leaders) to make the selection of who was to be released and who would be executed, hoping they would release Christ. To his utter amazement, they selected Barabbas to be released and Jesus to be executed. Thus again, Nisan 14 is plainly established. The Jewish people would never stand before Pilate on the High Sabbath of Nisan 15 and argue about who was going to be crucified on that day. It is also plainly established that since the Roman rulers wanted to please the Jewish nation, they would never have someone crucified on the High Sabbath of Nisan 15 in the first place. That would have been the most blatant affront to Judaism that the Romans could have made.

Another aspect of this situation should be emphasized here. This is the fact that Pilate had already designated other men to die on this day! It is **obvious** that he would not have designated them to die on the High Sabbath of Nisan 15. Thus, the day must have been Nisan 14.

7. **MARK 14:1, 2; LUKE 22:1, 2; MATTHEW 26:4, 5** "NOT on the Feast day [i.e., Nisan 15] lest there be an uproar of the people."

I want to emphasize the strength of this point by repeating it again. It was absolutely not their plan to have Christ killed on the High Sabbath of the Feast day. The reasons are given. They feared the people and they did not want a riot exploding in their faces. In this revelation, the Scriptures are actually telling us the secret fact of why the religious rulers pressed for the immediate death of Christ *before* the Passover. This is precisely why they were willing to stay up all night for the trial. They were not thinking of the Passover typology, but of their own safety. Nevertheless, by such fearful thinking they played a part in effecting God's timing that Christ die at the time of the sacrifice of the Passover lambs.

This is similar to the fact of why they did not break the legs of Christ in fulfillment of the Passover typology. It wasn't because the soldiers suddenly remembered the type of the Passover lamb. No! It was simply the fact that Christ gave up His life early, so that they didn't need to break His legs in order to hasten His death.

The fact that there is no revealed explanation as to why they would go ahead and allow Christ to be crucified on the Feast day against their own wishes, and that there was no riot among the people is, in and of itself, proof that Christ was not crucified on the Feast day of Nisan 15, as has been traditionally taught by Christendom.

8. **MATTHEW 27:62; MARK 15:42; LUKE 23:54; JOHN 19:42** (Please read each verse). All four Gospels are clearly united about the day on which Christ was crucified! "*. . . Because it was the Preparation Day, that is the day before the [High] Sabbath . . .*"

These verses are highly important because they show the actual positive **UNITY** of all four Gospel writers. All Four Gospel writers are *perfectly united* in saying that Christ was crucified on **"the Day of Preparation."** In no sense whatsoever could Nisan 15 ever be called "the Preparation Day." The simple fact that the 15th was the special High Sabbath of the Feast of Unleavened Bread totally excluded it from such a designation. This particular High Sabbath of Passover specifically had a day that was designated as the "Preparation Day." That was because, like no other High Sabbath, there was a great deal of work to be done in preparation for the special services on the 15th of Nisan: there was the cleansing of leaven from the homes, there were the special sacrifices of the Passover lambs in the afternoon of that day, and there was all the special preparation for that evening meal.

No one doubts that there is preparation done on Fridays for the regular, normal weekly Sabbath days. However, those Fridays are not specifically designated as "Preparation Days" in the Scriptures like Nisan 14. What preparation was done for the normal weekly Sabbaths always preceded the Sabbaths. However, if two Sabbaths ever occurred in succession, such as the Passover High Sabbath followed by a regular Sabbath, then the day before both Sabbaths was the "Preparation Day."

It is common knowledge that all the work done in preparation for the High Sabbath of Passover was done on the 14th day of Nisan. As stated before, this is illustrated for us in the days of King Josiah. They observed one of the greatest Passover celebrations in the history of the Nation of Israel (2 Chron. 35:18). Nisan 14 was specifically designated. Several times **"prepare"** or **"preparation"** is used of this day and one time the words, "make ready" (K.J.V.). See 2 Chron. 35:1, 4, 6, 10, 14, 15 and especially verse **16**. Thus Nisan 14 was called **"Preparation Day."**

The clear statements from all four Gospels are plainly devastating to the traditional "Good Friday" (Nisan 15) crucifixion of Christ. The 14th day of Nisan is plainly identified as "the Preparation Day" of Passover.

9. **JOHN 19:14** Not only does this passage say Christ stood before Pilate on "the Preparation [Day]," but it specifically says this day was "THE PREPARATION **OF PASSOVER**." In other

words this was the 14ᵗʰ Day of Nisan, the "Preparation Day for Passover." Words cannot be any plainer. The Scriptures are not at all ambiguous about this subject.

10. **JOHN 19:31** This passage illustrates what all the Gospel writers unite in telling us. They had to hasten the deaths of those being crucified so that they could take down their bodies and bury them before sunset which began the Sabbath. Lest anyone misunderstand what kind of a Sabbath this is, John was inspired to explain, "for that SABBATH DAY WAS AN **HIGH DAY.**" This means that the approaching day was the "High Sabbath" of Nisan 15, the actual first day of "the Feast of Unleavened Bread." Once again, this is very explicit language. There is absolutely no circumventing such clear testimony.

And again, in the beginning of the very same sentence, it is explained that this was "the Preparation" and the High Sabbath soon followed. These would all be very ludicrous statements if, as the traditionalists would have the Scriptures say, "Now they had Christ crucified on the High Sabbath because they didn't want to defile a regular Sabbath day." This would make the regular Sabbaths more holy than the High Sabbaths. Their doctrinal insistence has forced them to foolish confusion. And because most Bible teachers don't persevere in careful study, most of Christendom has been suffering some embarrassment for centuries.

## *Confusion over Sabbath Days*

When a text is read like Luke 23:54—"That day was the preparation, and the Sabbath drew near"—many assume that this means the regular Saturday Sabbath. Therefore, there is no question in their minds that Christ died on a Friday, the day before the Sabbath. This is good and fine IF the verse is referring to the regular Saturday Sabbath. *If,* however, it is talking about the special High Sabbath on the first day of the Feast of Unleavened Bread, then, as the expression goes, "we have a new ball game!"

Most chronologists of this event, either Jewish or Christian, recognize that there were *two different and distinct Sabbaths* in view at this Passover. Not only did the Law prescribe the regular seventh day Sabbath to be observed every week throughout the year, but it also prescribed the special "High Sabbaths" which occur during the various Feasts and Holy Days. There are actually seven such "High Sabbaths" which were held during the Mosaic year in connection with the three Feasts and special Holy Days. As I pointed out at the beginning of this study, during the Feast of Unleavened Bread there were two special "High Sabbaths." One such Sabbath was to be observed on the day after the sacrifice of the Passover lambs which was the first day of the Feast, i.e., Nisan 15. A second High Sabbath was to be observed on Nisan 21, the last day of the Feast.

The Law very clearly spelled out that the 14th day of Nisan was "the Preparation Day" for the "High Sabbath" of Passover (or Feast of Unleavened Bread) which began on Nisan 15. The Gospel of John tells us emphatically which Sabbath is in view at the death of Christ. John states "for that Sabbath was a *High Day*" (John 19:31).

Most chronologists of this event recognize that two different Sabbaths followed in succession on this occasion—first, the *High Sabbath* of Passover, which was on a Friday, and then, the regular seventh day *Sabbath*, which was on Saturday.

## Conclusion as to the Day Christ Died

I will allow these 10 specific Scriptures to stand as a perfect standard explaining the exact chronological day on which Christ died. These Scriptures also bluntly prohibit the traditions of apostate Christendom on this subject. They likewise demonstrate the absolute harmony and perfection of the Gospel records on the subject as to when Christ died.

These facts leave the supposed "super intelligent" humanist, agnostic, liberal, modernist, and all others who have loudly proclaimed "the Bible contradicts itself on this subject" in a very embarrassing position. Not only do the plain historical references testify to the fact that the Passover was observed in Palestine in Jesus's time an extra day, beginning on and including the whole of Nisan 14, but so also do three of the Gospel writers. Therefore we have found, after careful and full examination that the four Gospels stand in perfect harmony, unblemished and unblushing in truthfulness. The critics of the four Gospels have only displayed their ignorance about the correct Biblical teaching on this subject!

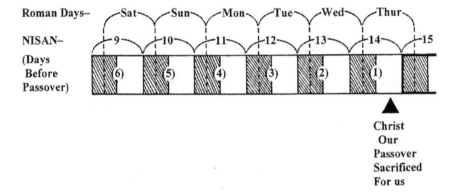

**Roman Days–**  Sat  Sun  Mon  Tue  Wed  Thur

**NISAN–**  9  10  11  12  13  14  15

**(Days Before Passover)**  (6)  (5)  (4)  (3)  (2)  (1)

▲
Christ
Our
Passover
Sacrificed
For us

# Chapter 4
# PERFECTION

## The Importance of the Slavery Issue

The Passover was first of all the *liberation* of the people of Israel from cruel Egyptian bondage. This was the primary purpose of the Passover event—to free the people of Israel in order that they might serve God in separation from the slavery and idolatry of Egypt. Because of this important aspect of its meaning the Jewish people also refer to the Feast as *"The Holiday of Freedom."* I saved a statement by a rabbi which illustrates this—

> The world today is searching for peace. Legend tells us that the month of Nisan, in which the festival of Passover occurs, which witnessed the redemption of the Jews from slavery in Egypt, will also witness their ultimate redemption, as well as the redemption of the entire world. And at that time, the world will be in a state of 'Koolo Shabbat'—a constant Sabbath, with Sabbath peace. We are all aware that Passover is the holiday of freedom, and freedom leads to peace. (Rabbi Zevulun Charlop, Jerusalem, Passover 1983)

Indeed, the spiritual significance of Passover is a reflection of that freedom. Egypt is a picture of the world which holds its slaves in the cruel bondage of sin. By means of the antitypical Passover Lamb, all who trust Christ are delivered from that bondage, with the prospect of serving God in separation and peace. As recorded in John 8:36 Jesus said, "Therefore if the Son makes you free, you shall be free indeed."

The two ingredients of the Feast which gave significance to the subject of Israel's bondage and slavery were the *bitter herbs* and the *unleavened bread*. The "bitter herbs" (Exo. 12:8) reflected on the fact that their lives were "made bitter with hard bondage" (Exo. 1:14). Moses indicated the "unleavened bread" also signified the fact that the people of Israel had eaten "the bread of affliction" for many years in Egypt (Deut. 16:3).

In addition, the prophets laid heavy emphasis on this aspect of the liberation of Israel from slavery. Moses said, "But the Lord has taken you and brought you out of *the iron furnace*, out of Egypt, to be His people, an inheritance, as you are this day" (Deut. 4:20). Solomon was reminded of this truth when he prayed to God "For they are Your people and Your inheritance, whom You brought out of Egypt, out of *the iron furnace*" (1 Kings 8:51). Isaiah spoke of God having "tested you (Israel) in *the furnace of affliction*" (Isa. 48:10). Jeremiah says ". . . in the day I brought them (Israel) out of the land of Egypt, from *the iron furnace*, saying 'Obey My voice . . .'" (Jer. 11:4). With language like this being used, it becomes evident that Israel's slavery was indeed very cruel with hard labor in the scorching sun of the Egyptian topography. No wonder the judgments of God upon Egypt were severe.

Many have stated, including President Lincoln himself, that the horrible desolation of our own Civil War in the 1860s (which was, no doubt, far more devastating than the judgments on Egypt) was a direct result of the judgment of God on the callous indifference of this country to the anguish of slavery. Indeed, Martin Luther King, Jr. capitalized upon the language of Scripture—"Let My people go"—in order to stir the hearts of this nation towards the "Civil Rights" movement just a few years ago.

Shall we not likewise be reminded that "Christ our Passover" was the basis for the liberation of the children of God from the horrible bondage of sin and death? Yes, the chief illustration in Paul's epistle to the Romans of the Christian's redemption is that of deliverance from our past life in sin's bondage to the glorious liberty of the children of God. In Romans chapter seven we see the picture of those "sold under sin" (Rom. 7:14), only able to do "what we (inwardly) hate" (v.15), while we are literally unable "to perform what is good" (v.18), "bringing one into captivity to the law of sin" (v. 23), so that we finally cry out "O, wretched man that I am! Who shall deliver me from this body of death?" (v. 24). The answer comes immediately, "I thank God—through Jesus Christ our Lord!" (v. 25). Therefore "the Spirit of life in Christ Jesus has made us free from the law of sin and death" (Rom. 8:2). As a result we are no longer "slaves of sin" (Rom. 6:6 and 17). "For we did not receive the spirit of bondage again to fear, but we received the Spirit of adoption by Whom we cry out, 'Abba, Father'" (Rom. 8:15).

Interestingly enough, on the night of Christ's last Passover supper with His disciples, after they had eaten of the customary feast meal, Christ spoke to them and said "No longer do I call you servants (lit., slaves), for a servant (lit., slave) does not know what his master is doing; but I have called you friends, for all things that I heard from My Father I have made known to you" (John 15:15).

In Appendix H I am going to include a letter I wrote in response to a vicious attack on the Bible over the slavery issue. Infidels often accuse the Bible of teaching and supporting the vicious slave trade industry. The Biblical facts are revealing. The whole Passover subject stands as a positive response to this attack on the Scriptures.

# Returning to the Daily Accounting

## NISAN 15

Matthew 27:62-66, "On the next day [Nisan 15]
which followed the Day of Preparation [Nisan 14], the chief
priests and Pharisees gathered together to Pilate . . ."

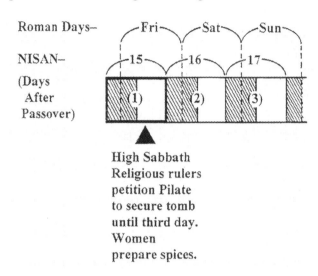

This was the first day after the crucifixion of Christ and after the regular Passover Feast had been eaten on the evening beginning this 15th day of Nisan. On the chart this is Friday of the Roman calendar day. The religious rulers had successfully delivered up Christ to Pilate the day before. Then they had piously eaten the regular Passover meal in the evening. Now, however, they had another immediate chore to perform. They are anxious that none of Christ's followers sneak in and steal away His body and make the claim of a resurrection of their Messiah. Therefore, on this day they appealed to Pilate for a guard of Roman soldiers to be dispatched to secure the tomb and prevent any such thing from happening. Again they were successful with their request. No doubt they smugly returned to their duties of this holy day thinking that this exasperating problem was finally over.

This is also the day in which the women, who had observed the place where the body of Christ was taken, made their preparations of spices and ointments (Luke 23:56). Though the High Sabbath Law strictly prohibited any public business or servile labor to be performed, yet regular household duties were allowed (Exo. 12:16 and Lev. 23:7, 8). On the regular Sabbath days even household chores were disallowed (Exo. 16:21-26 and Lev. 23:3). Thus, the women prepared these ingredients with the purpose of returning to the sepulcher after they had rested on the regular weekly Sabbath which followed this High Sabbath.

### NISAN 16

Luke 23:56; Matthew 28:1 and Mark 16:1, "And they rested on the Sabbath according to the commandment." "Now when the Sabbath had passed . . ."

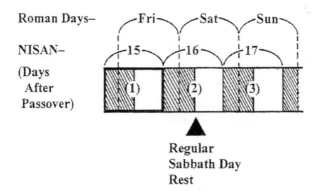

As was indicated earlier, one needs to distinguish between the High Sabbaths and the regular Sabbaths which were mandated for Israel. Most chronologists recognize that two Sabbath days followed in succession on this occasion. First, there was the High

Sabbath of the Passover itself—Nisan 15 (Friday). Then there followed the regular weekly Sabbath—Nisan 16 (Saturday). People who are not familiar with the distinctive High Sabbaths which occur on the special Jewish holy days often misunderstand some of the references using the term "Sabbath." The High Sabbath is in view in John 19:31, Mark 15:42 and Luke 23:54, where the body of Christ had to be taken down because the (High) Sabbath drew near. On the other hand, the regular weekly Sabbath is in view in Mark 16:1, Matthew 28:1 and Luke 23:56 where the disciples came to view the tomb. Of course, the traditionalists presume that nearly every one of these references is to the weekly Sabbath. Such is not the case.

## Three Days and Three Nights

It is appropriate now to discuss the time duration of Christ's death. There are many passages of Scripture that speak of Christ being raised from the dead *"after three days,"* or *"in three days,"* or *"on the third day."* Obviously, these must all mean the same thing though phrased differently—Matt. 16:21; 17:23; 20:19; 27:63; Mark 8:31; 9:31; 10:34; Luke 9:22; 13:32, 33; 18:33; 24:7, 46; John 2:19; Acts 10:40 and 1 Cor. 15:4. The normal understanding of all these expressions could fit only within the context of a Thursday crucifixion. The total time elapsing if Christ had died on a Friday afternoon would be less than one and three quarter days. If this were the case, then the normal expression would simply be "two days," or that Christ would be raised "the second day" after His death.

In addition to the previous expressions used, the Scriptures also make it plain that Christ's resurrection came within the context of a "three days and three nights" time period—see Matt. 12:40; 16:4; Luke 11:30 and Jonah 1:17. If these expressions are to be taken literally, then there are three daylight time periods and three nighttime periods involved in the expanse of time which elapsed from the death of Christ until His resurrection. Again, these expressions absolutely seal the doom of the idea of a Friday crucifixion death for Jesus Christ. A Friday crucifixion would involve only two daytime periods and two night periods.

The traditionalists usually try to harmonize all the statements with their Friday crucifixion by saying that these expressions are simply "Jewish idioms" in reckoning time. They point out that in some instances the reckoning of a "day" could mean only "a part of a day." No one actually denies that this is partly true, but everyone also knows that the Jewish idiom was not intended to evaporate whole days, either. The proper and normal Jewish idiom, were Christ to have died on the close of Friday and been raised early on Sunday morning, is simply "two days" and not "three days." The Scriptures would have said that He was raised from the dead on the second day after His crucifixion: Saturday being the first day after, and Sunday the second. However, if Christ died on a Thursday and was raised on Sunday morning, "three days" is the proper Jewish idiom.

With a Thursday crucifixion, the afternoon when Christ died would qualify for one daytime period because it was a sufficient part of that day. Friday supplies the second day period and Saturday supplies the third. Likewise, Thursday night supplies the first night, Friday the second and Saturday the third. Thus the only time of crucifixion which satisfies all the requirements of all the clear Scriptural statements is the death of Christ on Thursday afternoon. Even the traditionalists admit that a Thursday crucifixion would more naturally fit the requirements of Biblical language.

## NISAN 17

Luke 24:1 and 21, also Matt. 28:1; Mark 16:1; and John 20:1
"Now on the first day of the week, very early in the morning . . .
Indeed, besides all this, today is the **third day**
since these things happened."

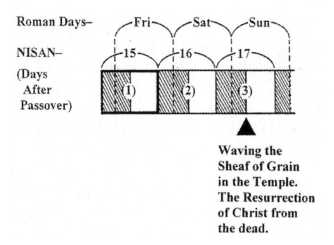

**Waving the
Sheaf of Grain
in the Temple.
The Resurrection
of Christ from
the dead.**

One final Scripture for our consideration, which adds confirmation to the foregoing facts, is found in Luke 24:13-27. Two of the disciples were walking on this Sunday away from Jerusalem, towards a little town named Emmaus. Their heads are throbbing in confusion and bewilderment at all that had recently happened. They had heard the reports that the tomb was found empty and that certain women had seen the resurrected Christ. This all sounded like idle tales to them. As they were walking along talking together none other than the resurrected Jesus, Himself, joined their company, but they were kept from recognizing Him. This stranger to them then asked, "What kind of conversation is this that you have with one another as you walk and are sad?"

They are provoked by this "stranger in Jerusalem" who seemingly did not know anything about the recent events. Consequently they explain what had recently happened to this "prophet, Jesus of

Nazareth." They finally told how He had been condemned to death and was "crucified" (verse 20). And then they add—*"and besides all this,* **TODAY IS THE THIRD DAY** <u>since</u> *these things were done."*

A more emphatic statement could not have been made. The ability to calculate when Christ was crucified is made easy for anyone. The translation is correct. That little word "since" is from the Greek word which literally translated means *"off from."* Now if this Sunday was the **Third** day since (*off from*) the crucifixion, then going backwards we can observe that Saturday was the **Second** day since (*off from*) the crucifixion and Friday was the **First** day since (off from) the crucifixion. That makes <u>Thursday the crucifixion day</u>! This confirms the results of all that we have studied so far.

Some have tried to understand Christ's death as occurring on a Wednesday. I will explain why the idea of a Wednesday crucifixion is not realistic in Appendix B.

## The Offering of the Omer

We have seen that Christ fulfilled the Passover typology to absolute perfection in two major aspects chronologically—that of the Selection of the Lamb, and that of the Sacrifice of the Lamb. Now there is a third aspect to this typology. Interestingly enough, probably some of the very priests who had condemned Christ were busy early this Sunday morning also. They were busy at the Temple in the ritual performance of another highlight in the Feast of Unleavened Bread. This had to do with the waving up in the air the handful of freshly cut firstfruits of grain as a very special offering to God, symbolizing the dedication of the whole Firstfruit harvest to God. The waving of the sheaf of grain served as a *guarantee* or token of the greater harvest which would be celebrated 50 days later. In addition, of course, we know that this special offering also symbolizes resurrection—the very RESURRECTION of Jesus Christ from the dead. So, in the

Temple the priests were performing a ritual which demonstrated the resurrection of Christ, yet they turned around in a few moments and offered a bribe to deny the fact of Christ's resurrection (Matt. 28:11-15).

This particular ritual could only be performed by the Children of Israel once they had arrived in the Land of Promise (Lev. 23:9). This was called "the Offering of the Omer" or "the offering of the Firstfruit Wave-sheaf" of grain. This was a handful of early grain or a bundle of sheaves of grain which was to be waved up in the air. In their wilderness journey there were no grain fields to be found in the desert. When they came into their land they inherited many grain fields and became farmers of the land. This special offering added an agricultural flavor to the whole Passover event, and made it the first of what came to be called "The Three Agricultural Feasts" of Israel: one, Passover; two, Pentecost or Feast of Weeks; and three, Tabernacles or Ingathering. The Offering of the Omer (handful or sheaf) after Passover served as a token of the greater spring harvest to come. That Spring Harvest Feast was to be celebrated seven weeks or 50 days after the Offering of the Omer. Hence, it was called the Feast of Weeks, or later—Pentecost (50th). The Fall Harvest Festival was the third Feast.

Of special interest to us right now is this first grain offering, the Offering of the Omer—the Wave-sheaf of Firstfruits. The law concerning it was given to the people of Israel in Leviticus 23:9-14. One must remember that the immediate context for these instructions concerning the "Wave-sheaf" is the Feast of Unleavened Bread, Lev. 23:4-8. Therefore, it is to be understood that this law had to do with a new thing which would be practiced at a specific time during the Feast of Unleavened Bread, when the Children of Israel came into the Promised Land. The instructions read (Lev. 23: 10, 11)—

> . . . you shall bring a sheaf [omer or handful] of the
> FIRSTFRUITS of your harvest unto the priest. He shall

WAVE THE SHEAF BEFORE THE LORD, to be accepted on your behalf; on the <u>DAY AFTER THE SABBATH</u> the priest shall wave it.

## *Another Heated Controversy*

The interpretation of the timing of this offering was the subject of heated controversy in early rabbinic times. Before Christ was born, the Sadducees prevailed in controlling the priesthood and the Temple services. They continued to hold control until about 20 years before the destruction of the Temple by the Romans in A.D. 70. Thus, the Sadducees controlled the Temple services for some twenty years after the death of Christ and the founding of the Christian Church (see Acts 4:1; 5:17). Politically, the Sadducees were in good standing with the Romans, but during the last 20 years of the Temple the Pharisees came to be in control and many things changed, including the day on which the "Omer" was offered.

Now the Sadducees were well-known for their very liberal beliefs and rejection of certain fundamental truths, such as a literal resurrection of the dead and the existence of angels, spirits, etc. (see Acts 4:1-2 and 23:8). However, they were also surprisingly conservative or literalists in some aspects of interpreting the Law. In fact, the Sadducees held only to the written Law of Moses and rejected the various traditions of the Pharisees. The Pharisees, on the other hand, were the highly orthodox group that went even beyond the written Law to observing their "Oral Law" (traditions) as equal authority. Their oral laws sometimes contradicted the written Law. This became the major difference between the two groups, and the major difference in the observance of the "Offering of the Omer." This difference had to do with the time in which it was to be offered.

The day on which the Pharisees would observe the offering eventually prevailed in practice after they gained control. It still does until this time in the Jewish world. The Pharisees were actually looking to assign some historical event in Israel's early history to the celebration of the Feast of Pentecost. Unlike Passover and Tabernacles, which were attached to the Passover lambs in Israel's deliverance from Egypt, and to their dwelling in booths (tabernacles) for forty years, Pentecost was named only by the number of days from the Offering of the Omer—seven "Weeks" (Hebrew, Shavuot), or Pentecost (50th). Therefore since the giving of the Law occurred some 50 days after Israel's exodus, they assigned Pentecost to the commemoration of the giving of the Law. The Pharisees took the word "Sabbath" in Lev. 23:11 to mean the special High Sabbath of Nisan 15 and thus the Offering of the Omer would always be done on the following morning of the 16th of Nisan. (See *The Jerusalem Post, International Edition*, Rabbi Reskin, "What's in a name?" June 1, 2006, and "Something doesn't add up," May 21, 1999, and the June 6, 2003 article.)

Please remember, the Offering of the Omer marked the beginning of "the counting of days" (Lev. 23:15, 16) until Pentecost. Now Moses went up on mount Sinai approximately 50 days after Israel left Egypt on the 15th of Abib. Therefore, historians believe that the Pharisees took this position in order to correlate the Feast of Pentecost with the giving of the Law from Mount Sinai approximately fifty days after the first Passover in Egypt. In so doing, they converted Pentecost into a Feast which would commemorate the giving of the Law, which in its Biblical setting is not specifically stated nor actually indicated.

However, as I stated before, at the time of Christ's death the Sadducees were still very strongly in control of the Temple services and the priesthood. They rejected the oral law of the Pharisees, including this attempt to change the nature of Pentecost and the time of the Offering of the Omer. They were known to take the passage in Leviticus literally and thus, since the word "Sabbath" was not designated as the "High Sabbath," the Sadducees said it was simply the regular Sabbath which would fall during the Feast of Unleavened Bread. Therefore, the Omer would always be offered on a **Sunday** *morning* after the regular Sabbath which occurred during the feast. This, likewise, would mean that Pentecost, which followed seven weeks later, would also fall on a Sunday.

At the time of Christ, this meant that on Sunday morning when the priests were making this particular Wave Offering before the Lord in the Temple services, the disciples were hearing the news of Christ's resurrection from the dead. And shortly thereafter the Roman soldiers were offered bribes and protection by the religious rulers to change their story (see Matt. 28:11-15).

In this regard, I would have to agree with the position of the Sadducees as do certain scholars today. The historical references for most of this I have taken from: *The Pentateuch & Haftorahs*, edited by J.H. Hertz under "the Omer," pages 520, 521; *The Encyclopedia Judaica*, under "Sadducees" and "Shavuot" (Weeks or Pentecost); *Guide to the Jewish Holy Days* by Hayyim Schauss, pages 87, 88; *Davis Dictionary of the Bible*, "Weeks, feast of," page 809, and other articles such as I listed above from *the Jerusalem Post, International Edition*.

## *Significance of the Wave-sheaf of Firstfruits*

In the Greek Scriptures the inspired apostle Paul makes it very plain that Christ's Sunday morning resurrection was in fulfillment of the "Firstfruits" offering (See 1 Cor. 15:20, 23 and Rom. 8:11, 23). Thus again, we can rest assured that at the time of Christ, the Offering of the Omer took place on Sunday morning.

As to the interpretation of the meaning of the offering, I would also take a literal approach and allow the Scriptures to speak for themselves. In this ritual offering there are several major ingredients for us to look at—

**First**—The initial planting of the kernels of grain serves as a picture of death. Christ said as recorded in John 12:24, *"Truly, truly, I say unto you, except a kernel of wheat fall into the ground and **DIE**, it abides* *alone: but if it die, it brings forth much fruit."* Christ said this in regards to His death. The apostle Paul repeated this same truth.

**Second**—The springing up of the new stalks of grain speaks of resurrection from the dead. *"If it die, it brings forth much fruit,"* Christ said. The apostle Paul said in 1 Cor. 15 (the great resurrection chapter in the Bible) verses 35-38, *"But someone will say, 'How are the dead raised up? And with what body do they come?' Foolish one, what you sow is not made alive unless it dies. And what you sow, you do not sow that body that shall be, but mere grain—perhaps wheat or some other grain. But God gives it a body as He pleases, and to each seed its own body."* How beautiful and strong this argument is! Whenever one is in the countryside and looks out on the abundant fields of grain, it should be remembered that all this sparkling new life came out of what appeared to be *death*—cold, hard kernels planted into the ground.

**Third**—In the ritual offering, a sampling of this first harvest in its early form is called *"the Firstfruits"* (Lev. 23:10). Again, Christ's words indicated that in His resurrection He would *"bring forth much fruit"* (John 12:24). And again, the divinely inspired apostle Paul leaves no doubt in one's mind as to the meaning. *"Christ is risen from the dead, and become the FIRSTFRUITS of them that slept"* (1 Cor. 15:20). Paul repeated it again for emphasis—*"Christ the FIRSTFRUITS"* (verse 23).

**Fourth**—As we have seen so far, this typology is clearly identified as a picture of Christ in resurrection. However, Christ was not just raised from the dead. He also *ascended* into the Heavens to His Heavenly Father. Thus, what happens as the major action of this particular offering is the **manner** in which it is offered. This handful of grain isn't burnt on the altar, nor is any of it spilt out beside the altar. It is not dropped on the ground or set down in pots or pans, nor is it merely held out with the hands. No! None of these things! It is beautifully and wonderfully **waved up in the air** as if it could just *ascend* into heaven itself. This waving of the grain up in the air is said to be done *"before the LORD"* (Lev. 23:11). In other words, it is intended to picture going up to God. This offering actually belongs to the Lord. Since the Lord does not actually reach down and take the grain, therefore only the priests as God's representatives were to take it for themselves after it was waved up to God. The waving up in the air is clearly the picture of **ascension.** Sometime after Christ arose from the dead, the Scriptures say *"He ascended to the Father"* (John 20:17; Acts 2:32-35; Eph. 4:8, 9; Psalm 68:18).

**Fifth**—This handful of grain stood as a token or *guarantee* of the greater harvest to be celebrated fifty days later. So vital was this connection that they, therefore, counted the weeks and days (Lev. 23:15, 16) until the Pentecostal spring Harvest Feast. Some Jewish commentators even call Shavuot (Weeks or Pentecost) "the eighth day of the Feast of Unleavened Bread" because of its vital connection to the Offering of the Omer. The most popular name given to the Feast of Pentecost is "Feast of Weeks of Firstfruits." (See Exo. 23:16; 34:22; Lev. 23:17 and Num. 28:26.) The Offering of the Omer was the *token* "Firstfruits" of the spring "Harvest Feast of Firstfruits."

## The Vital Connection

There is, therefore, a **most vital** connection between this handful of green or early grain and the greater spring harvest to be celebrated 50 days later. The first offering was typical of the resurrection and ascension of Christ. It was designed to stand as a sampling of the later Pentecostal offering in **both resurrection and ascension** as well. Therefore, the Pentecostal ritual, which is also waved up in the air in a similar manner, is actually prophetic of the same events of resurrection and ascension as was the earlier sample. This fact is missed by most Bible teachers simply because the Church was born on Pentecost Day and therefore they think that Pentecost was somehow only prophetic of the birth and nature of the Church. Such is only partially true (see my Bible study, *The Pentecostal Rapture of the Church*).

The fact is, the Church of Jesus Christ was born on a day which was prophetic in typology of the Church's resurrection and ascension—i.e., **the Rapture.** Again, the apostle Paul makes this very plain when he said, *"Christ the firstfruits, then **they that are Christ's** at His coming"* (1 Cor. 15:23). In other words, what happened to Christ as the "Firstfruits" in resurrection and ascension is a picture of what will happen to all those who belong to Christ at His coming for them, i.e., their collective resurrection and ascension. Please remember that in the Pentecostal offering the full ripe grain has now been ground into "fine flour," kneaded together in one large batch "with leaven," divided into "two loaves," and "baked" for "firstfruits to Jehovah" as a "wave offering" (Lev. 23:16-20). This is called *"a New Grain Offering"* (Lev. 23:16). It is not the purpose of this study to expand upon this beautiful picture. Needless to say, it is breathtaking in mystery and beauty as the meaning is later unfolded in the epistles of Paul. (See also Romans 8:11 and 23).

So it is, that while some of the chief priests and elders were shocked by the soldiers' account of the events at the tomb, and therefore were urgently offering large amounts of money to the soldiers to change their story for the sake of the general public (Matt. 28:11-15), yet they had to turn right around and participate in the services of this special "Offering of the Omer." Customarily at that time it was the first thing in the morning of this first day of the week that they solemnly enacted all its rituals in the midst of great pageantry of praise and prayer. Perhaps this is what led to the conversion of a large number of priests as stated later in Acts 6:7. No doubt, they would be remembering the divinely inspired symbol befitting the reality.

Thus, we conclude our journey. We have seen that Christ fulfilled the Passover typology to absolute perfection in its three major chronological aspects: the *Selection of the Lamb*, the *Sacrifice of the Lamb* and the *Offering of the Omer*. We have also seen that the four Gospel accounts are splendidly accurate, whereas the skeptics, who have loudly proclaimed contradictions in the record of Christ's death and resurrection timetable, suffer the embarrassment which is fitting to their prejudicial clamor.

On the next page is a large chart that will place all these events together.

## THE END

*Jack W. Langford*

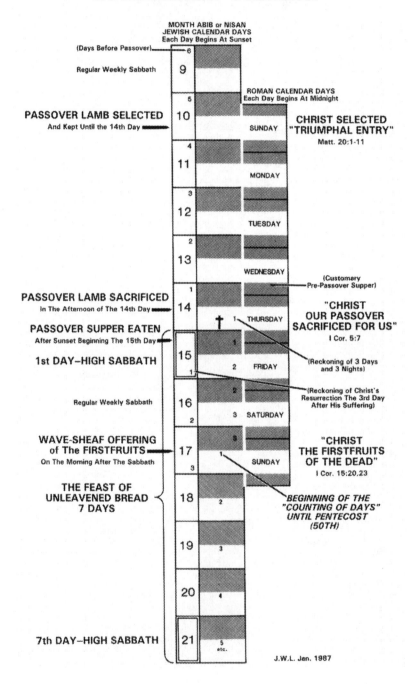

**CHRIST'S DEATH AT THE PASSOVER**
As It Took Place In A.D. 30 -- A CHRONOLOGY

MONTH ABIB or NISAN
JEWISH CALENDAR DAYS
Each Day Begins At Sunset

(Days Before Passover)

Regular Weekly Sabbath — 9

ROMAN CALENDAR DAYS
Each Day Begins At Midnight

**PASSOVER LAMB SELECTED**
And Kept Until the 14th Day — 10

**CHRIST SELECTED**
**"TRIUMPHAL ENTRY"**
Matt. 20:1-11

SUNDAY

11 — MONDAY

12 — TUESDAY

13 — WEDNESDAY

(Customary
Pre-Passover Supper)

**PASSOVER LAMB SACRIFICED**
In The Afternoon of The 14th Day — 14 — THURSDAY

**"CHRIST
OUR PASSOVER
SACRIFICED FOR US"**
I Cor. 5:7

**PASSOVER SUPPER EATEN**
After Sunset Beginning The 15th Day

**1st DAY—HIGH SABBATH** — 15

(Reckoning of 3 Days
and 3 Nights)

FRIDAY

(Reckoning of Christ's
Resurrection The 3rd Day
After His Suffering)

Regular Weekly Sabbath — 16 — SATURDAY

**WAVE-SHEAF OFFERING**
of The FIRSTFRUITS — 17
On The Morning After The Sabbath

SUNDAY

**"CHRIST
THE FIRSTFRUITS
OF THE DEAD"**
I Cor. 15:20,23

**THE FEAST OF
UNLEAVENED BREAD
7 DAYS** — 18

*BEGINNING OF THE
"COUNTING OF DAYS"
UNTIL PENTECOST
(50TH)*

19

20

**7th DAY—HIGH SABBATH** — 21

etc.

J.W.L. Jan. 1987

76

# Appendices

## APPENDIX A

### *The Use of the Word "Evening."*

It could be confusing for beginning students of this subject to understand the meaning of "evening of the 14th day" (Exo. 12:6 and Lev. 23:5). In the original Mosaic reckoning, the total 24 hour day period begins with the evening. "The evening and the morning were day one" (Gen. 1:5, etc.). However, sometimes Moses would also call the close of a day its "evening." Therefore, the question has been asked, "Is it the beginning 'evening' of this day which is in view, or the closing 'evening' which is in view?" A few religious groups argue seriously over this point.

Here are illustrations of the word "evening" being used for the close of a day, especially where important days and rituals are in view. In Leviticus 23:27 we are told that "the *tenth* day of this seventh month is a Day of Atonement . . . a Holy Convocation [or High Sabbath]." Then in verse 32 we are given the exact perimeters of that Day of Atonement (the 10th) in the following manner: "In the *ninth* day of the month *AT EVENING*, from *evening* [of the 9th] to *evening* [of the 10th], shall you celebrate your Sabbath [the Day of Atonement]." Since this Holy Day is the 10th day, we recognize that the expression "the ninth day of the month at evening" must mean the "evening" that closes the ninth day and not the evening that would begin the ninth day. Otherwise, the Day of Atonement would be on the 9th and not on the 10th. Likewise, the "evening" that closes the 10th day is meant.

Another example is in Numbers 28 (see also Exo. 29:38-41). In this chapter, verses 1-8, we have the institution of the Daily Sacrifice which was to be offered at a specific time each day. However, since the "Daily Sacrifice" was twofold (that is, two sacrifices were to be offered each day), we are given the time of day as to when these two sacrifices were to be made. Every day during the daylight hours there would be two sacrifices offered, the first one in the *"morning"* hours and the second one in the *"evening"* hours of that same day. "Evening" in this case obviously means the close of the day. Jewish history concerning the Temple services is in agreement with this. The Daily Sacrifices were offered twice daily, first in the morning (usually by 9:00 A.M.), and then in the late afternoon hours (usually no later than 5:00 P.M.).

Concerning the actual order of events at the first Passover in Egypt, we can place together the following sequence, which further proves that the Passover was sacrificed in the afternoon closing the 14th day:

1.  Before the Passover actually occurred, the people of Israel had already spoiled the Egyptians. In Exo. 11:2 God told Israel to ask of the Egyptians of their silver and gold. The next verse (3) tells us that Israel received "favor in the sight of the Egyptians." That means the Egyptians gave of their substance to Israel. This is confirmed for us in Exo. 12:35, 36. The people of Israel had already "borrowed of the Egyptians . . . and they spoiled the Egyptians."

2.  Then the people of Israel were to actually eat the Passover dinner that night "with belts on their waists, sandals on their feet, and staffs in their hands, and in haste . . . for in this same day I will

have brought your armies out of the land of Egypt" (Exo. 12:11, 17). In other words, the people of Israel were to eat this supper being fully ready to travel the first thing in the morning because *"that day"* they would be leaving Egypt. This, of course, was the 15th day.

3. Because the children of Israel had to leave Egypt "in haste" they did not have time to leaven their dough and allow it to rise. Therefore, the tradition of eating unleavened bread started.

4. That night, when all the households of the Egyptians were struck with the death of the firstborn son of each family, there arose a great cry in Egypt. Pharaoh rose up that night and called Moses and told him to take the Israelites out of Egypt immediately. Likewise, during the remaining hours of that night, the Egyptians were urgent upon the Israelites to leave lest the whole nation of Egypt perish (Exo. 12:29-33).

5. "On the *fifteenth day* of the first month, on *the morrow* [daylight hours] *after the Passover*, the children of Israel went out [of Egypt] with boldness in the sight of all the Egyptians . . . for the Egyptians were burying all their firstborn" (Num. 33:3, 4).

Since the people of Israel left Egypt on the morning of the 15th day, after having eaten the Passover supper the previous night, it is evident that the original expression—"In the first month, on the 14th day of the month AT EVENING"—means the evening which closes the 14th day (Exo. 12:6, 8, 18) and not the evening that began that day.

# APPENDIX B

## *A Wednesday Crucifixion?*

Some Bible teachers have sincerely tried to arrive at an absolutely full three 24 hour time periods passing from the death of Christ until His resurrection. Of necessity they would have Christ crucified on

Wednesday afternoon. There are several insurmountable difficulties prohibiting this conclusion.

To insist that the time of Christ's death until His resurrection as taking "three days and three nights" must mean that there were exactly 72 hours involved is actually changing the calibration of the inspired text. One should never convert this expression of "three days and three nights" into how many actual "hours" Christ spent in the grave. None of the texts say how many actual hours Christ spent in the grave. How many "hours" is a different calibration and an actual distraction from the facts stated. We must only believe that three daytime periods and three nighttime periods were involved in the duration of Christ's death. Obviously a Friday crucifixion violates these expressions because only two daytime and two nighttime periods would be involved.

Since Christ died in the afternoon, and these teachers feel the need of an absolute full three days and three nights passing before His resurrection, then Christ would of necessity have been raised in the afternoon of the third day at the exact same time that He died three days before. This day could not have been Sunday afternoon because the text plainly says He had risen by early morning of that day. Therefore, they move the time of crucifixion back to Wednesday afternoon and say that Christ had actually risen from the dead about *sunset* on Saturday and He simply did not appear to anyone until Sunday morning.

This is the second problem with that scenario. It makes Christ appear to no one for at least 12 hours after His resurrection. Such a conjecture does not fit the tenor of the Biblical account of the resurrection. To have Christ raised on Saturday evening does not sound as odd as it really is. Those who propose this view usually measure the total time of Christ's death from His *burial in the tomb* on the close of the day He died instead of from the time He actually died on the cross. Therefore, they would say He arose "three days" later on Saturday evening. The Biblical facts are that the time period of the three days and three nights is not to be measured from His *burial in the tomb*, but from His death in the afternoon and immediate descent into Hades for three days and nights (Acts 2:31; Eph. 4:9; Matt. 12:39, 40). Remember that Jonah was another prophetic type of Christ. In this case, Jonah was in "Sheol" or Hades for three days and three nights (Jonah 1:17 and 2:2), not a tomb. Thus, if their logic is to be followed completely, and they were to use the actual Biblical stipulations, then Christ must have risen from the dead on Saturday afternoon—about three in the afternoon, three days after He physically died. This is even more embarrassing because it now has Christ raised from the dead approximately 16 hours before He appeared to anyone. This is obviously even more out of line with the Biblical account.

In addition, with a Wednesday crucifixion it is a plain fact that Friday would be a regular workday in which the women, having prepared the burial ingredients in their homes on the High Sabbath of Thursday or on Friday morning, could normally have come to the tomb in time to finish the procedure of Christ's burial. This, obviously, did not happen. In light of all the foregoing material, a Wednesday crucifixion simply does not harmonize.


# APPENDIX C

## *What is the Actual Historical Date of Christ's Death?*

Most chronologists, both religious and secular, now agree that it was during the Passover of A.D. 30 Why is this? Our present calendar method of dating from the birth of Christ did not begin until the sixth century when the pope adjured that the calculations of one Dionysius Exiguus be accepted as the standard for Christendom and the world. More careful historical studies have proven that these calculations are incorrect. His alignment with certain events of Roman history, such as the death of Herod the Great, has proven to be four years in error.

Interestingly enough, the present pope, Benedict XVI, acknowledges this correction to the date of Christ's birth in his most recent book— *The Infancy Narratives of Jesus of Nazareth*, December 2012.

As we know from the Bible, Christ was born while Herod the Great was living (see Matt. 2:20-22). The Jewish historian Josephus precisely identifies the year of Herod's death as there occurred a lunar eclipse just before his last illness (Josephus, *Antiquities of The Jews*, XVII.6.4). In giving this clue, Josephus also gave the modern scientist something to work with in order to positively confirm this date. Thus, this eclipse has now been astronomically identified as indeed occurring on the date of March 12, 4 B.C. just a few weeks before the death of Herod.

Sometime before Herod died he attempted to destroy all the babies of Bethlehem two years old and under. This age limit was not because he thought the child was two years old, but was to guarantee the death of the infant Who would later claim to be King. Other Biblical facts would indicate that Christ was probably born in September/October of 5 B.C. (calculations from the month Zacharias served in the Temple—Luke 1:5; 1 Chron. 24:10 and Neh. 12:17). Consequently, Christ began His public ministry at 30 years of age in late A.D. 26. There are other facts of the Biblical record, cross related to secular historical dates, which seem to be in agreement with this. His ministry lasted for about three and a half years until early A.D. 30. And thus, He was crucified at the time of the Jewish Passover, on the 14th day of Nisan, in the spring of A.D. 30 (April 6th, to be exact by the reckoning of some according to today's calendar.)

Within the last 30 years there have been computer calculations of the new and full moons of past antiquity. Several of these have noted that in A.D. 30 the Jewish Passover (which is governed by the lunar calendar) involved two Sabbaths falling in succession, the 15th (Friday) and 16th (Saturday) of Nisan. Thus, the Passover of that year came on a Thursday evening—Nisan 14/15 (April 6th.) as most generally understood by chronologists today. See especially the notations by Roger Rusk (emeritus professor of physics at the University of Tennessee), *"The Day He Died," Christianity Today,* March 29, 1974.

## APPENDIX D

## *Historical Support for a Thursday, Nisan 14, Crucifixion.*

Historical support for the Nisan 14 crucifixion of Christ comes from at least three sources:

1. A very early Jewish source was the "Tractate Sanhedrin" in the *Babylonian Talmud* which recorded with generally understood reference to the Founder of Christianity: "On the Eve of Passover Yeshu [Jesus] was hanged." (Sanhedrin 43a GBT VII, pg.181; SBT pg.281).
2. The very early Apocryphal *Gospel According to Peter* also states this same conclusion, that Jesus was delivered to the people "on the day before the Unleavened Bread, their Feast" (Verse 3). This is talking about the regular 7 day Feast from Nisan 15 through Nisan 21.
3. The "Quartadecimanian Controversy," culmination at the Council of Nicaea A.D. 325. Some further explanation of this should be made—

As was stated at the beginning of this study, many of the "Eastern (Asia Minor) churches" from very early times had been celebrating a sort of "Christian Passover" on Nisan 14. They called it "Pasch." I need to explain that at first this had to do with the suffering and crucifixion of Christ. Later they seemed to add to it His resurrection as well. This is where the word "Quartadecimanian" comes from. It simply means the "14th." This tells us that they believed Christ was crucified on the 14th at the time of the sacrifice of the Passover lambs. And therefore, they contended that this day was to be kept in remembrance by them from the very times of the apostles themselves. The largest faction, the "Western church (centered in Rome)," was called "Quintodecimans," which simply means the number 15 (of the Month Nisan). They wanted to celebrate either or both the crucifixion and resurrection on the 15th. Quite a dispute followed. Most believed that only a Sunday should be set aside to celebrate the resurrection. The Council of Nicaea finally settled the argument by simply decreeing the observance of a Sunday resurrection of Christ, calling it "Easter" as was already somewhat customary, and setting the date as we explained before. The main purpose in doing this was to divorce their celebrations from the Jewish Passover.

(See *The History of the Christian Church from Christ to Constantine*, by Eusebius, approx. A.D. 330, Dorset Publishing, 1965, pgs. 222-234; *"Pessah and Easter: the Christian Perspective"* by Malcolm F. Lowe, *Jerusalem Post*, April 13, 1991; *Encyclopedia Britannica*, 1954, "Easter;" *The Evangelical Dictionary of Theology*, Baker, "Easter;" and *The New Catholic Encyclopedia*, on Easter, etc.)

## APPENDIX E

## Relationship of the Offering of the Wave-sheaf (Omer) of Firstfruits to the Feast of Pentecost 50 days later.

Once when I gave a two-part public message on this subject of the day on which Christ died (Los Angeles, March 10th, 1991), I included with it several charts on overhead transparencies. I thought it would be helpful to include in this material the one chart which illustrates this relationship between the two Feasts.

As explained earlier (see page 73, *The Vital Connection*), the offering of the Wave-sheaf of Firstfruits (also called the Omer) served as the early token *Firstfruits* of the later spring Harvest of Firstfruits to be celebrated 50 days later. The later Harvest Feast celebration had a "Wave Offering" as well. In this case it was in the form of *two loaves of bread* being "waved" in the air. As a result of Christ being "our Passover" Who was sacrificed, buried and *gloriously resurrected* (being waved in the air) on our behalf, the Church of Jesus Christ was born 50 days later. The actions which took place on this Feast Day of Pentecost (waving the two loaves of bread in the air) spoke of our guaranteed hope of also being resurrected with Him. Thus the Church of Jesus Christ was actually born on a **prophetic** feast day—prophetic of resurrection and ascension (i.e., what we commonly call "the Rapture"). We can therefore say, **"When the antitypical Day of Pentecost *is fully come*, we will all be of one accord, in one place."**

On the chart, the 1ˢᵗ day is marked with an asterisk (*) to indicate this as the Sunday upon which our Savior arose from the dead. And this is the day upon which the "Wave-sheaf of the Firstfruits" of grain was offered. 50 days later (also marked with an asterisk) was Pentecost Sunday when the two loaves of bread were offered by being waved in the air as well.

Note the following chart which visually demonstrates the relationship between the Wave Offering of Firstfruits and the Feast of Pentecost—

Sunday, * Christ Risen, "Offering of the Omer,"
The "Counting of Days" begins.

| Sun. | Mon. | Tues. | Wed. | Thur. | Fri. | Sat. | (Sabbaths) |
|------|------|-------|------|-------|------|------|------------|
| *1. | 2. | 3. | 4. | 5. | 6. | 7. | 1. |
| 8. | 9. | 10. | 11. | 12. | 13. | 14. | 2. |
| 15. | 16. | 17. | 18. | 19. | 20. | 21. | 3. |
| 22. | 23. | 24. | 25. | 26. | 27. | 28. | 4. |
| 29. | 30. | 31. | 32. | 33. | 34. | 35. | 5. |
| 36. | 37. | 38. | 39. | 40. | 41. | 42. | 6. |
| 43. | 44. | 45. | 46. | 47. | 48. | 49. | 7. |
| *50. | | | | | | | |

7 Sabbaths = 7 Weeks or 49 Days,
Sunday, *50 a High Sabbath, "Pentecost" (50th),
"Feast of Weeks" or "Feast of Firstfruits."

## APPENDIX F

### Principal Passages from the Hebrew Scriptures— on the Subject of the Passover

1. Exo. 11 and 12:1-51—the institution of the first Passover in detail.
2. Exo. 13:1-16—to be taught to all future generations.
3. Exo. 23:14-17; 34:18, 23—all males to appear before the Lord 3 times a year, beginning at Passover.

4. Lev. 23:1-44—High Sabbaths distinguished from regular Sabbaths. 7 High Sabbaths a year. Institution of the Wave–sheaf Offering of grain.
5. Num. 9:1-14—no bones of the Passover lamb to be broken. Law for unclean persons to observe Feast a month later. Order for discipline.
6. Num. 28:16-25—various offerings for the seven days of the Feast.
7. Num. 33:1-3—Israel leaves Egypt on morning of Nisan 15 after Passover meal the night before.
8. Deut. 16:1-8—Lamb is sacrificed in the afternoon (of 14th). No meat left after the meal. The lamb is to be sacrificed only where God places His Name once Israel arrives in the Land.
9. Joshua 5:10, 11—Joshua's Passover.
10. 2 Chron.30:1-27—Hezekiah's Passover.
11. 2 Chron.35:1-19—Josiah's Passover.
12. Ezra 6:19-22—Ezra's Passover.

# APPENDIX G

## *Principal Examples of the Three Days*

1. Gen. 22:4, 5—Isaac (see also Heb. 11:19).
2. Gen. 42:16-18—Joseph.
3. Exo. 3:18—Israel.
4. Exo. 15:22-25—bitter waters.
5. Exo. 19:10, 11—Israel sanctified.
6. Num. 19:11, 12—purification.
7. 1 Sam. 30:11-13—captive revived.
8. 1 Kings 12:5, 12—Rehoboam.
9. Jonah 1:17—Jonah.
10. Esther 4:15-5:1—Esther.
11. Hosea 6:1-3—Israel restored.

12. Luke 13:32, 33—Christ's work.


## APPENDIX H

## *Slavery—Israel's Deliverance from Bondage in Egypt and the Law Regarding Slavery*

### *Slander Against the Biblical Position on Slavery*

Another area where the infidel tries to attack the Bible is in the area of slavery. I read such an attack in the very popular "Free Inquiry" magazine back in 1987. A supposedly knowledgeable professor gave a typical tirade against the Biblical account. I would like to include in this Appendix my letter of response to that article. Though the editor of "Free Inquiry" thanked me for my letter, the author of the article, Professor Morton Smith, made no response. Apparently he was not interested in truth, but was only repeating things he had heard. There are similar attacks made by infidels on this subject. I hope the following material will cause you to better appreciate the truth of the Bible on a very popular world custom regarding the issue of slavery.

April 23rd, 1987
2854 Milam
Fort Worth, Texas
76112

Paul Kurtz
Editor, Free Inquiry
3159 Bailey Ave.
Buffalo, N.Y. 14215

Dear Mr. Kurtz,

The recent article by Morton Smith which represents the Bible's position on slavery lacked honest objectivity, showed a biased attitude and was a very unbalanced presentation. Allow me to illustrate what I mean—

1. The very first thing represented was that the Bible "prescribes it (slavery) for a whole third of mankind." Mr. Smith cites the curse placed upon one of Noah's sons (Ham) as proof. The real facts are: a) Noah's three sons fathered 17 sons between them—one of whom was named Canaan. The prophetic curse was placed upon Canaan. At best, this would represent 1/17 of the human race; b) The Canaanites, however, were a very small number of people who later inhabited the "Land of Canaan." Geographically, Canaan is about the size of the state of New Jersey; c) It is common knowledge among Bible students that the curse was fulfilled when the "Children of Israel" conquered the Canaanites and put them to servitude. As you can see, this is an infinitesimally small fraction of the human race.

   The publication of this exaggeration by Morton Smith only serves to qualify you as good "Humanistic-Pentecostalists!" You have had some excellent articles exposing the stupid exaggerations of modern "Faith Healers." Then, you turn around and do the very same thing, yourselves, in a futile effort to discredit the Bible.

2. Many scholars and historians have long recognized that the Law of Moses, as it regards slavery, was revolutionary in its time. Israel had, in fact, been a slave people. They had come out of a bondage in what they properly called "the Iron Furnace" of Egypt—see Deut. 4:20. All their legislation, therefore, was aimed for the protection and well-being of slaves, and they were reminded of their bondage as these laws were delivered—Deut. 15:15. In addition, fully 1/3 (and this is no exaggeration) of the tribes of Israel were produced by the servant and/or slave wives of Jacob. The unusual high regard for slaves will immediately become obvious to the reader of the Hebrew laws. After the Ten Commandments, the very FIRST laws of social order were for the protection of slaves!

3. Any Israelite who became involved in stealing and selling human beings was subject to the <u>DEATH PENALTY</u>. Exo. 21:16 says, "He that stealeth a man, and selleth him, or if he be found in his hand, he shall surely be <u>put to death</u>."

4. Any Israelite who beat a slave so as to cause his death would be subject to the DEATH PENALTY as if he had murdered a free man. Exo. 21:20 says (Morton Smith failed to translate this properly), "And if any man smite his servant (slave), or his maid (slave) with a rod, and he die under his hand; <u>HE SHALL SURELY BE AVENGED!</u>" Under the Mosaic judicial system retribution by an "Avenger" always meant DEATH.

5. If a slave was even accidentally killed by an ox or other animal, the master or owner of the animal would be fined 30 shekels of silver and the animal was put to death—Exo. 21:32.

6. If a master so much as knocked out a tooth of a slave—that slave was automatically set free—Exo. 21:26, 27.

7. If a master loved a female slave and had sexual relations with her, he was fully obligated to perform the duties of marriage as if he had married a free woman. This was binding upon him even if he decided he did not love her. He was prohibited from selling her, and if he failed to fully support her as lawfully married, then she was automatically set free—Exo. 21:7-11 and Deut. 21:10-14.

8. Any Hebrew person who was forced into voluntary slavery was to be treated as a "hired servant" (Lev. 25:40), was automatically set free after six years of service (Exo. 21:2) and was given a bountiful payment at the time of his release (Deut. 15:12-15).

9. The Law of Moses fully protected all runaway slaves—Deut. 23:15, 16. Any slave who was to flee into the land of Israel had the right to choose any place where he wanted to live, and he was fully guaranteed to never suffer any kind of oppression. Israel literally became a haven for runaway slaves.

10. Furthermore, all existing slaves in the land of Israel, regardless of whether they were Hebrews or foreign born, were automatically inheritors of all the covenant blessings promised by Jehovah for

the nation—see Gen. 17:1-14 and 17:22-27. In addition, they worshipped side by side with their masters—see Genesis 14:14 as an example.

In conclusion, it is obvious from laws like these (most of which were left out of Mr. Morton Smith's article) that the idea of slavery was altogether different in Israel than in any other nation. This is one of the reasons the translators of the Hebrew Scriptures found it difficult to render the word slavery in an intelligible way for other societies. It has well been said, "a bond slave in Israel was better off than a hired servant in other countries."

Those who have tried to make the Bible countenance the form of slavery which was practiced in the United States of America before the Civil War (and that is 3500 years after the Law of Moses was written) have long been effectively answered. Were they to have implemented the Law of Moses on the subject of slavery into the American legal system in the early 1800s, it would have spelled the DOOM of the slave trade industry and there never would have been the bloody Civil War to leave such a horrible memory for this modern nation.

Messianic prophecies of both the Hebrew and Greek Scriptures speak of a new social order in the age to come. Under the rule of Messiah there will be a full liberation of all mankind who enter that time of bliss. In the interim, a rabbi named Paul, who converted to Christ, appealed to all Christian slaves to submit to their masters and do good service as unto Christ. He also warned Christian masters that one day they will face their Master—so treat their slaves accordingly. Likewise, he repeatedly showed the equality of masters and slaves in the sight of God—1 Cor. 7:21, 22; Gal. 3:28; Col. 3:11. The peace and rest that this spiritual logic brought was incalculable. The expressions "SERVANT" and "MASTER" as found in the Greek Scriptures became such noble words that they were chosen to become the legal terminology used in all jurisprudence in "Employer-Employee" relationships in the English speaking world.

Sincerely Yours—a servant of Christ,
Jack W. Langford

(As a further footnote, it should be stated that the primary provisions of the Law of Moses regarding slavery in the land of Israel pertained to Israelites themselves, who had sold themselves into a form of bondage to other Israelites in order to pay off their debts. Not all these laws, therefore, necessarily pertained to foreigners who were taken captive in warfare. In many cases slavery was the alternative to being annihilated. Of course, slavery of these Gentile peoples was most often merely a very loose form of control. The people were often allowed their own cities and farms.)

## APPENDIX I

### *Slavery, Letter of Liberation*

To this subject can be added *The Epistle of Paul The Apostle to Philemon.* Here is the shortest of Paul's fourteen letters. And yet this letter is a power-packed liberation message to a Christian owner of a slave. The apostle Paul, under divine inspiration, used spiritual diplomacy in the name of the Lord Jesus Christ to gain not merely the freedom, but also the equality of this slave.

One of the sad facts of American history is that when our Civil war was over, though the black man was technically set "free," he had no equality and was so badly treated that many of the ex-slaves thought their condition was better under slavery. The government could free the slaves but it could not change the hearts of its citizens. In Paul's letter of liberation he not only presents the truth of freedom but most importantly he presents the truths that melt the heart.

Onesimus was a runaway slave who somehow met Paul who was himself in chains in Rome. Now the Roman empire engaged in the slave industry more than any other nation or empire in world history. Some historians calculate that half the people in the capital of the Roman empire were slaves. However, under the gentle evangelism of Paul, Onesimus was saved and became a Christian very close to Paul's heart. Now Paul was sending him back to his owner.

Under Roman law Onesimus could have been put to death.

Under the "Law of the Spirit of Life in Christ Jesus" Onesimus got life, liberty and equality. Notice the sequence of this man's liberation—

First, Paul acknowledged that at one time Onesimus was considered an unprofitable slave (verse 11). That was before his conversion.

But now in Christ, Onesimus is dear to Paul's "own heart" (verse 12).

In addition, Onesimus was serving Paul, as if he were Philemon himself (verse 13).

Paul appealed for Philemon to "voluntarily" consider Onesimus free (verse 14).

Paul also appealed to Philemon to receive Onesimus as if it were "forever" (verse 15), no longer as a slave but as a beloved brother (verse 16).

Paul further appealed to Philemon to consider Onesimus as he would his own person and even as he would consider Paul, himself (verse 17).

All that Onesimus might owe was to be placed on Paul's account; he would repay it (verse 18, just as Jesus Christ has done for every sinner).

Now to the infidel, I would challenge, "You find a more liberating document than this letter! And I give you permission to search all the literature of all the history of all mankind on the face of all this earth!"

In our own United States of America, when the "Emancipation Proclamation" was issued during the Civil War, the whole world gave its approval and praise. However, by no stretch of the imagination did the black man receive the same equalities in every sphere with the white man—not even for many years to come. In contrast, in Paul's inspired proclamation the slave Onesimus was to be regarded by his previous master as he would regard his own person, and even as he would regard the apostle Paul, himself. In fact, Onesimus was to be regarded as a fellow brother in Christ for all eternity.

The subject of the Passover is the subject of the liberation of a nation in slavery. All the Hebrew Scriptures can be looked upon from this perspective. The subject of the antitypical Passover, in the person of the Lord Jesus Christ, is again the subject of liberation from the awful gloom of universal slavery. This is the very heart of what we call the New Testament. In this regard the Bible is a very liberating book. The prophetic aspect of both the Hebrew Scriptures and the Greek Scriptures looks forward to that great Jubilee of final redemption from both the physical and spiritual aspects of the bondage of sin.

## APPENDIX J

### *Pope Benedict XVI, Recent Declaration and Book*

As I stated at the end of my foreword to this study, the pope's very recent declaration that Christ probably ate the Passover Supper "a day early" and then died at the actual time of the sacrifice of the Passover lambs is quite astonishing, especially in the light of the long past history of Christendom's dedicated observation of the popular "Good Friday" crucifixion event. If Christ ate the Passover a day earlier without a Passover Lamb then He also died a day earlier at the exact time those Passover lambs were being sacrificed. That means Christ did not die on so-called "Good Friday," but rather on Thursday. We can ask the question, "Has it really taken 1682 years to correct the error of the so-called 'fathers' at the Council of Nicaea in the year A.D. 325?" As I stated in this study, I am glad that I Have found certain Bible teachers who came to this conclusion long ago on the basis of what the Bible itself had to say under careful scrutiny. This was true in my own investigation as well. Nevertheless, I will herein give important excerpts from the pope's address exactly as it was published in *The Wanderer*.

> VATICAN CITY (*ZENIT*)—Here is the homily Benedict XVI delivered Thursday, April 5, 2007 for the Mass of the Lord's Supper, celebrated in the Basilica of St. John Lateran.

*ZENIT* is an independent news agency which specializes in the translation and publication of the pope's messages and other materials from the Vatican. *ZENIT* made the following translation of Benedict XVI's homily entitled "Jesus Is The New And True Lamb". I am only going to quote a very small portion of that homily as translated.

> In the narrations of the evangelists, there is an apparent contradiction between the *Gospel of John*, on one hand, and what, on the other hand, Matthew, Mark, and Luke tell us. According to John, Jesus died on the cross precisely at the moment in which, in the Temple, the Passover lambs were being sacrificed. His death and the sacrifice of the lambs coincided.

> This means that He died on the eve of Passover, and that, therefore, He could not have personally celebrated the paschal supper; at least this is what it would seem.

> On the contrary, according to the three synoptic evangelists, the Last Supper of Jesus was a paschal supper,

in its traditional form . . . This contradiction, until a few years ago, seemed impossible to resolve.

The Pope continued to explain how the discovery of the Qumran manuscripts has led us to a "convincing possible solution that, while not accepted by all, is highly probable." He has therefore come to the conclusion that the Gospel of John "is historically correct" and that Jesus actually died "on the eve of Passover at the hour of the sacrifice of the lambs." Then he goes on to state—

> . . . He [Christ] celebrated Passover with His disciples probably according to the calendar of Qumran, that is to say, at least one day earlier—He celebrated without a lamb, like the Qumran community who did not recognize the Temple of Herod and was waiting for a new Temple.

Benedict XVI went on to say twice more that Jesus celebrated the Passover "without a lamb," other than His own Body and Blood as the "Lamb of God."

All this is taken from *The Wanderer,* Vol. 140, No. 16, April 19, 2007, "Pope's Holy Thursday Homily . . . 'Jesus Is The New And True Lamb'"

I appreciate the pope expressing his conviction about this important event. And I certainly agree with his major conclusion. However, I do not believe that the Qumran calendar had anything whatsoever to do with the issue. The facts are—as I have presented in this study—it was customary for the Jewish people at the time of Christ, and until this very day in Israel, to eat a Feast meal on the evening beginning the 14th day of Nisan, which meal commemorates the sacrifice of those lambs in the afternoon of that day. In addition, and primarily, the overwhelming abundance of united Scriptural evidences forces us to the conclusion that Christ died at the time of the sacrifice of the Passover on Thursday.

# Catholic Answers

As an additional matter of interest, I wrote an inquiry to Tim Staples of *This Rock Magazine* which is produced by the *Catholic Answers* organization (letter dated May 3rd, 2007). Tim Staples is an "Apologist" for Roman Catholicism in that organization. Mr. Staples was so surprised by my representation of what the Pope had stated that he just couldn't believe it.

Staples did some extensive research of his own and wrote me back over a month later (letter, June 13th, 2007). Mr. Staples' main conclusion was that "The good folks at Zenit.org mistranslated the text" of Benedict XVI's message. He made many suggestions to alleviate the possibility that the "Church" could have been wrong all of these years and finally said that I needed to read the translation from "the Vatican website . . . [and] find the proper translation."

This translation was made by *Libreria Editrice Vaticana*. I found and read carefully the translation which was made directly from the Vatican. I immediately notified Tim Staples (e-mail letter dated June 17, 2007) that this translation essentially said the very same things that the Zenit.org translation stated. This obviously frustrated Mr. Staples.

In further response, Mr. Staples could only make some very confusing assertions in an attempted explanation (e-mail, dated June 18, 2007). Finally he concluded—

> But I would ask the question: who are we to correct the Church in her tradition throughout the centuries? . . . I don't know about you, but I do not believe I am competent to correct the Church in her liturgical prayer and in her belief over the centuries. I am called to defend it. Tim Staples, Staff Apologist, Catholic Answers.

# New Catholic Encyclopedia

Herein is, in all probability, an accurate and true representation of the source for Benedict XVI's assertions in his homily. The *New Catholic Encyclopedia*, 1967, Vol. 10, pages 1071 and 1072, on the subject of the Passover states what many Catholic scholars have now come to believe. You will note that it is essentially the same conclusion the Pope suggested in his homily—

> The Synoptics represent the Last Supper as a paschal [Passover] meal . . . though none of the Evangelists mentions the lamb. However John places the Supper on the evening before the Preparation Day, i.e., 24 hours before the Jews ate the Passover . . . This problem has received no completely satisfactory solution. Since it is now known that the Qumran community had a different calendar, it is possible that Jesus celebrated the Passover on a different day than official Jewish usage. He may have performed the paschal rite without using a lamb that had been ritually immolated in the Temple.

# The Pope's Latest Book

In April of 2007 I had only the "News Flash" of the pope's statement and then the exact text of it as was printed by *The Wanderer*. Now, four years later, we have the actual book published by Ignatius Press—*Jesus of Nazareth, Holy Week: From The Entrance Into Jerusalem To The Resurrection,* by Pope Benedict XVI, 2011. In reading the pope's discussion of the chronology of this week I was surprised to see how much he depends upon other investigators instead of his own research.

As to the day upon which Christ died, the pope finally discarded the theory centered around the use of the Qumran calendar. He said, "Jesus is unlikely to have used a calendar associated principally with Qumran. Jesus went to the Temple for the great feasts" (page 111). The pope then settles upon a classic work by John P. Meier, *A Marginal Jew: Rethinking the Historical Jesus,* which he believes explains the chronology of a Thursday crucifixion the best. As if choosing between John and the Synoptic Gospels, the pope says—

> John is right when he says that at the time of Jesus' trial before Pilate, the Jewish authorities had not yet eaten the Passover and, thus had to keep themselves ritually pure. He is right that the crucifixion took place, not on the feast, but on the day before the feast. This means that Jesus died at the hour when the Passover lambs were being slaughtered in the Temple. That Christians later saw this as no coincidence, that they recognized Jesus as the true meaning of the ritual of the lambs—all seems to follow naturally. (Page 112.)

And of course, the pope could very well add as a result of this disclosure, that we now know the Roman Catholic Church, and all the rest of Christendom which has chosen to follow it, has been celebrating the wrong day in the wrong way, and causing horrible confusion and slander against the Scriptures for the last 1700 years.

In the end, though the collection of religious confusion needs to be exposed, the Word of God remains the same throughout the ages. The truth manifested therein actually becomes brighter each and every day—*"there is a spirit within man, and the inspiration of the Almighty gives him understanding"* (Job 32:8).

—THE END—

# GENERAL INDEX

## A

Abraham, xx

## B

Babylonian Talmud, 14, 34, 83
Benedict XVI, Pope, xxi, 3, 94
    *Jesus of Nazareth–Holy Week*,
      xxii, 98
    *Infancy Narratives of Jesus of*
      *Nazareth, the*, 82
Bishop, Jim,
    *Day Christ Died, the*, ix

## C

*Catholic Answers*, 97
Charlop, Zevulun, Rabbi,
    Jerusalem, Passover 1983, 59
Chag ha-Matzoth, 18
Chag he-Aviv, 18

## D

*Davis Dictionary of the Bible*,
    Feast of Weeks, 71

## E

Easter, x, xiii, xiv, 2, 3
Easter Month, 4
Edersheim, Alfred,
    *Life and Times of Jesus the Messiah*,
      12, 34
*Encyclopedia Britannica*,
    Easter, 84
*Encyclopedia Judaica*,
    Shavuot, 71
Eusebius,
    *History of the Christian Church*
    *From Christ to Constantine*, 84
*Evangelical Dictionary of Theology*,
    Easter, 84
evening, 78
Exiguus, Dionysius,
    *calculations*, 81

## F

Feast of Unleavened Bread, 6
Festival of Redemption, 1
fig tree cursed, 28
Firstfruits, 8
Foundation Compendia Rerum
    Iudaicarum ad Novum

# SCRIPTURE INDEX

# GREEK SCRIPTURES

## Matthew
Matt. 2:20–22, *82*
Matt. 12:1–8, *22*
Matt. 12:40, *64, 81*
Matt. 16:4, *64*
Matt. 16:21, *64*
Matt. 17:23, *64*
Matt. 20:19, *64*
Matt. 21:9, 15, *24*
Matt. 21:17–25:46, *29*
Matt. 22:15, *30*
Matt. 22:15–22, *30*
Matt. 22:23–33, *30*
Matt. 22:34–40, *30*
Matt. 22:41–46, *30*
Matt. 26:1–5, *30*
Matt. 26:4, 5, *54*
Matt. 26:5, *33*
Matt. 26:6–16, *32*
Matt. 26:17, *42, 46*
Matt. 26:17–19, *12*
Matt. 27:62, *38, 48, 54*
Matt. 27:62–66, *62*
Matt. 27:63, *64*
Matt. 28:1, *63, 64, 66*
Matt. 28:11–15, *68, 71, 74*

## Mark
Mark 8:31, *64*
Mark 9:31, *64*
Mark 10:43, *64*
Mark 11:1–11, *24*
Mark 11:9, 10, *24*
Mark 11:11–18, *28*
Mark 11:19–20, *29*
Mark 11:27–33, *29*
Mark 11:27–12:37, *29*
Mark 14:1–2, *30, 33, 54*
Mark 14:3–11, *32*
Mark 14:9, *32*
Mark 14:10, *33*
Mark 14:12, *10, 42, 44, 46*
Mark 14:12–16, *12*
Mark 15:42, *45, 48, 54, 64*
Mark 15:42–43, *37*
Mark 16:1, *63, 64, 66*

## Luke
Luke 1:5, *82*
Luke 9:22, *64*
Luke 11:30, *64*
Luke 13:32, 33, *64, 87*
Luke 18:33, *64*
Luke 19:40, *25*
Luke 20, 21, *29*
Luke 22:1, *7, 17*
Luke 22:1–2, *54*
Luke 22:1–6, *32*
Luke 22:7, *10, 43, 45, 46, 48*
Luke 22:7, 15, *46*
Luke 22:44, *27*
Luke 23:54, *37, 48, 54, 56, 64*
Luke 23:56, *63, 64*
Luke 24:1, 21, *66*
Luke 24:7, 46, *64*
Luke 24:13–27, *66*
Luke 24:32, *xi*

## John
John 1:29, 36, *25*
John 2:19, *64*
John 3:1–21, *xvi*
John 3:16, *25*
John 5:18, *33*
John 7:1, 19, 25, *33*
John 8:36, *60*
John 8:37, 40, *33*
John 11:1–45, *23*
John 11:57, *28*
John 12:1, *21*
John 12:1–8, *23*